MORMON
FAITH *in* AMERICA

MAXINE HANKS
WITH **JEAN KINNEY WILLIAMS**

J. GORDON MELTON, SERIES EDITOR

®

Facts On File, Inc.

MORMON FAITH IN AMERICA
Faith in America

Facts On File, Inc.
132 West 31st Street
New York NY 10001

Library of Congress Cataloging-in-Publication Data

Hanks, Maxine, 1955-
        Mormon faith in America / Maxine Hanks.
            p. cm. —(Faith in America)
        Includes bibliographical references and index.
        ISBN 0-8160-4991-2 (alk. paper)
            1. Church of Jesus Christ of Latter-day Saints—United States—History.
            2. United States—Church history. I. Title. II. Series.
        BX8611.H292 2003
        289.3'73--dc21   2002156383

Facts On File books are available at special discounts when purchased in bulk quantities for businesses, associations, institutions, or sales promotions. Please call our Special Sales Department in New York at (212) 967-8800 or (800) 322-8755.

You can find Facts On File on the World Wide Web at http://www.factsonfile.com

Produced by the Shoreline Publishing Group LLC
Editorial Director: James Buckley Jr.
Contributing Editor: Beth Adelman
Designed by Thomas Carling, Carling Design, Inc.
Photo research by Laurie Schuh
Index by Nanette Cardon, IRIS

Photo and art credits: Cover: Corbis (main image); AP/Wide World (3).
AP/Wide World: 16, 20, 26, 39, 63, 67, 80, 82, 90, 92, 93, 98, 103, 106; Corbis 29, 55, 68, 76, 112; Courtesy Brigham Young University Art Museum 6, 24, 34 (with permission from and thanks to Jeannette Holmes); Courtesy of the Church Archives, The Church of Jesus Christ of Latter-day Saints 11, 32, 36, 42, 47, 50, 58, 73, 88, 101, 116.

Printed in the United States of America

VB 10 9 8 7 6 5 4 3 2 1

This book is printed on acid-free paper.

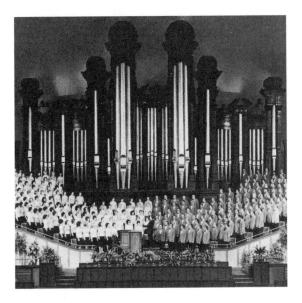

CONTENTS

FOREWORD

AMERICA BEGINS A NEW MILLENNIUM AS ONE OF THE MOST RELIGIOUSLY diverse nations of all time. Nowhere else in the world do so many people—offered a choice free from government influence—identify with such a wide range of religious and spiritual communities. Nowhere else has the human search for meaning been so varied. In America today, there are communities and centers for worship representing all of the world's religions.

The American landscape is dotted with churches, temples, synagogues, and mosques. Zen Buddhist zendos sit next to Pentecostal tabernacles. Hasidic Jews walk the streets with Hindu swamis. Most amazing of all, relatively little conflict has occurred among religions in America. This fact, combined with a high level of tolerance of one another's beliefs and practices, has let America produce people of goodwill ready to try to resolve any tensions that might emerge.

The Faith in America series celebrates America's diverse religious heritage. People of faith and ideals who longed for a better world have created a unique society where freedom of religious expression is a keynote of culture. The freedom that America offers to people of faith means that not only have ancient religions found a home here, but that newer forms of expressing spirituality have also taken root. From huge churches in large cities to small spiritual communities in towns and villages, faith in America has never been stronger. The paths that different religions have taken through American history is just one of the stories readers will find in this series.

Like anything people create, religion is far from perfect. However, its contribution to the culture and its ability to help people are impressive, and these accomplishments will be found in all the books in the series. Meanwhile, awareness and tolerance of the different paths our neighbors take to the spiritual life has become an increasingly important part of citizenship in America.

Today, more than ever, America as a whole puts its faith in freedom—the freedom to believe.

Mormon Faith in America

Founded by a young prophet from the American frontier, the Church of Jesus Christ of Latter-day Saints (whose members are often called Mormons) emerged in the 20th century as a global faith. Its members are now found in more than 200 countries. The young missionaries who go from door to door introducing people to their faith have become some of the world's most recognizable religious adherents. In country after country Mormon temples have arisen to mark the faith's coming of age.

Unique among religions, their continuing journey began in the United States. Latter-day Saints first appeared in upstate New York in the 1820s, where Joseph Smith, Jr. told people about his visions of God and a new revelation delivered into his hands by an angel. Following the publication of the Book of Mormon, people gathered around Smith and followed him to settlements in Ohio, Missouri, and Illinois, where in 1844 their prophet was murdered. A new leader, Brigham Young, emerged to lead them west to a new land, now known as Utah. Over the next generation Mormons spread across the West, creating new settlements and offering their faith to Native Americans and the new settlers alike.

Controversial through the 19th century, not least because church members practiced polygamy, the Mormon Church experienced a new beginning in the 20th century. This was signaled by their abandonment of their unique family system, statehood for Utah, and the election of the first congressmen and senators from the new state.

Since that time, Mormons have moved to accommodate their life to American culture and to integrate their religious community into the diversity of American faiths. *Mormon Faith in America* introduces this unique American-born and -bred faith and its many contributions to American life and history.

— *J. Gordon Melton, Series Editor*

INTRODUCTION

Mormon Beliefs and Practices

THE MORMON FAITH WAS FORMED BY A TEENAGED BOY NAMED Joseph Smith, Jr. (1805–1844), who declared a new vision of God and scripture in the 1820s. His name was plain and he taught a simple idea—that anyone can talk to God and get answers. His new scripture, the Book of Mormon, proclaimed the heavens were open with new revelations for God's children.

Many people believed immediately in Smith's visions and scripture, and millions joined the religion he started. The story of that religion is now embodied in the Church of Jesus Christ of Latter-day Saints (LDS)—whose members are known as Mormons—and its story is the story of how a 14-year-old boy founded a worldwide religion.

In 1844, not long after Smith proclaimed the beginnings of the Mormon church, Josiah Quincy, the mayor of Boston, wrote in his 1883 book *Figures of the Past*, "It is by no means improbable that some future textbook, for the use of generations yet unborn, will contain a question something like this: What historical American of the 19th century has exerted the most powerful influence upon the destinies of his countrymen? And it is by no means impossible that the answer to that interrogatory may be thus written: Joseph Smith, the Mormon Prophet."

Uniquely American Origins

Most religions in America came from other countries, but Mormonism did not migrate here or land on this shore. The Mormon faith was born in the American culture of the 1700s and 1800s. It is a home-grown faith that came out of the American frontier like new crops sprouting in fertile soil. To understand the origins of the LDS Church, though, one must look earlier, at the birth of the American culture and nation. The religion Smith founded came out of the same background that created America.

The early settlers of New England were Puritans, who practiced a form of Protestant Christianity and who came seeking religious freedom in the 1600s. Puritans wanted to restore what they called the "pure" Gospel of ancient Christianity. They believed they were God's chosen people, the elect who would build a New Jerusalem or City of Zion. As God's "covenant people" (people who had a special agreement with God), as they were known, they were devoted to establishing the kingdom of God—a community that would embody God's will. Their society would conform to their theology and the Bible, and their government would be an unfolding of religious truth. Anyone who did not conform to God's will (as they saw it) would be expelled. Puritans valued religious freedom to create their own society, but they did not tolerate those who did not share their views.

The Puritan New England culture of the 1600s and 1700s greatly influenced the birth of the LDS Church in the 1820s. The earliest Mormons were raised on Puritan culture, seeing both its potential and its demise. As Puritanism died out in the late 1700s, Mormonism was born amid its ghosts.

Independent Nation, Independent Religion

In the 1820s, when Smith was starting the LDS Church, the United States was a new country, not quite 50 years old. The generation from 1760 to 1800 won independence and laid the foundations for a government based on a key set of freedoms: freedom to speak, worship, work, and live according to one's personal beliefs. Joseph Smith's parents were of that generation—his father, Joseph Smith, Sr., was born in 1771, and his mother, Lucy M. Smith, was born in 1775.

Most Americans of the post-Revolution era did not want a single dominant religion or a state church, such as those in Britain and the nations of Europe. Americans wanted freedom of belief. In 1776, fewer than 10 percent of Americans belonged to a church, and in the 1820s, fewer than 20 percent. The vast majority of Americans were not members of an organized religion. Into this open environment came sweeping religious movements, seeking to turn Americans into Christians. (From 1776 to 1845, the American population grew 10 times, from 2.5 million to 20 million people, yet the number of Christian preachers grew 22 times, from 1,800 to 40,000.)

The Great Awakening (1730–1750) was a Christian religious movement that took hold of the American colonies and kindled a Puritan revival of the calling to God's salvation.

The Second Great Awakening (1790–c.1830) reached out to settlers scattered on the frontier, in places such as western New York and Pennsylvania, Ohio, Kentucky, and Tennessee. This movement made salvation available to all—through human choice or free will. Revivals, or camp meetings, urged people to receive God immediately through prayer and conversion. Preachers emphasized participation by everyone, not just ordained ministers.

Both Awakenings focused on a personal relationship with God, and on the restoration of the pure Gospel (that is, not the Gospel as interpreted by churches) of ancient Christianity. The Great Awakening highlighted God's power—to restore and establish His kingdom; the Second Awakening later in the century highlighted the human ability to agency—that is, to bring God's true church into being. The birth of the Mormon religion was influenced by both Awakenings and united their most compelling ideas in one faith. The most prominent idea of all was the Restoration.

THEOLOGY
A system of religious thinking; the beliefs of a religion.

Restoration and Reformation

The Restoration Movement believed that the Protestant Reformation of the 1500s in Europe had fallen short. The Reformation tried to bring back a purer Christianity by reforming the Catholic Church and creating the Protestant faiths. Yet, Restorationists felt the Reformation had failed to restore original Christianity. Restorationists believed that only God or Christ could restore the "true" Christian Church.

This restoration movement was sweeping New England in the early 1800s when Joseph Smith was born in Vermont in 1805. Smith's parents and grandparents were devout Restorationists who fully believed in a restoration of God's pure religion. Smith's father "would not subscribe to any particular system of faith, but contended for the ancient order, as established by our Lord and Savior Jesus Christ, and his Apostles," wrote his mother Lucy in the 1853 book *Lucy's Book*. She also urged her family to seek the "true church," and find it "whether it was in the Bible or where ever it might be found even if it was to be obtained from heaven by prayer and Faith."

Smith was born just before Christmas on December 23, 1805, in Sharon, Vermont. He was the third of seven sons among 11 children, and his family had lived in New England for several generations.

In his mid-teens, Smith divulged to his family and others that he had seen a vision of God in 1820, and that an angel had visited him several times from 1823 to 1827.

These visions garnered some attention in New England, where religious visions were taken very seriously. But Smith met with public hostility when he reported in 1827 that he had received "gold plates" from an angel. And he rocked religious society when he—an unschooled farmer—published the Book of Mormon, a complex, 500-page book of scripture, when he was only age 24. The book was said to have been inspired by God, with the gold plates being used as a sort of code-breaker that enabled Smith to decipher the word of God, as given to him by the angel. Smith's book captivated many people who were seeking a Restoration, and it convinced them that his visions were real. Smith continued to report visionary experiences almost constantly for 25 years, from age 14 to age 38. During this time, he said, heavenly beings gave him instructions and the power to bring forth an entire religion.

What Is the Mormon Faith?

The religion practiced by the LDS Church is not a Protestant denomination nor is it the result of the Reformation or a protest, but, as it says in the Book of Mormon, "restoration to the earth of the original Christian Church, which fell into apostasy [division and departure from a true Church belief] during the early centuries of the Christian era."

This restoration was based on the testimony of Smith, who said that God and Jesus Christ appeared to him personally in 1820, "calling me by name." Smith inquired of them, as reported in the Book of Mormon, "which of all the sects was right—and which I should join. I was answered that I must join none of them, for they were all wrong."

A holy place
This is the Sacred Grove near Palmyra, New York, believed by Mormons to be the place where Moroni gave the golden plates to Joseph Smith, Jr. It is a popular destination for Mormons exploring the roots of their faith.

Smith said he was was called by God to restore the true Christian Church, "the only true and living church upon the face of the whole earth." Smith published the Book of Mormon and organized the Church of Christ in 1830, which was renamed Church of Jesus Christ of Latter-day Saints in 1838. People who believed in the Book of Mormon and joined the new church were called Mormons.

Mormonism is a Christian faith which centers its doctrine on Jesus Christ as the means of salvation for all humankind. Mormonism was founded on two premises: restoration and revelation. God restored His true Church, and He revealed His will to a prophet—Joseph Smith. Mormons believe that the Church of Jesus Christ of Latter-day Saints is the literal restoration of the original Christianity established by Jesus Christ 2,000 years ago.

God's Kingdom in America

Just as America declared independence from Great Britain in 1776, the Mormons declared their independence from other religions in 1820. Smith said in the Book of Mormon that God "established the constitution of this land" and chose America for the restoration of the Gospel. The Mormon Church was a new version of Christianity that dared to restore the "kingdom of God" in America, and prepare the world for Christ's return.

Smith taught in *The Book of Doctrine and Covenants* that the Church was "the restoration of all things spoken by the mouths of all the holy prophets since the world began." The religion is a melting pot, where many traditions came together in a new way, created in 19th-century America from both ancient and contemporary elements. Mormonism includes many elements from both the Jewish and Christian traditions, both the Old Testament and the New Testament of the Bible. It captures the spirituality of the American frontier and the Old World, including mystic traditions.

Living Prophets—Foundation of the Faith

The faith of the LDS Church is based on the idea of a prophet, a visionary person who can communicate with God. This notion comes from the Old Testament, where prophets such as Moses, Isaiah, and Daniel talked with God and received answers, which they recorded as scripture. Mormons believe that prophets did not cease with the Old Testament, but still exist today, known as "living prophets" or "modern prophets." Mormons believe Smith is the first prophet called by God in modern times.

Yet a prophet does more than have visions and talk with God. A prophet also has followers who believe him. A prophet and his followers interact, creating a social movement. Mormonism grew from one person to 26,000 people in its first 14 years. After Smith died in 1844 (see page 31), the faith continued winning new converts across America and other countries, and still attracts new members today.

Today the LDS Church is the fifth largest church in America, with 6 million members in the United State and 5 million more scattered around the globe. A 2002 survey by the Glenmary Research Center found that the Mormon faith was the fastest-growing religion in America, growing by about 19 percent from 1990 to 2000.

MORMON

The name Mormon comes from the name of a character mentioned in the Book of Mormon. He is supposed to be an ancient historian who was the original author of some parts of the book translated by Joseph Smith, Jr.

Mormon Scriptures

The LDS Church as an organized religion developed as Smith began to put his visions into form and practice. The revelations of Smith and other early Mormon leaders became scripture, theology, doctrine, priesthood, sacred rites, beliefs, church structure, and practices. The faith

Mormon Articles of Faith

This is the list, written in 1842 by Joseph Smith, Jr., of beliefs that all members of the Mormon Church must follow:

1. We believe in God, the Eternal Father, and in His Son, Jesus Christ, and in the Holy Ghost.

2. We believe that men will be punished for their own sins and not for Adam's transgression.

3. We believe that through the atonement of Christ all men may be saved, by obedience to the laws and ordinances of the Gospel.

4. We believe that these ordinances are: First, faith in the Lord Jesus Christ; second, repentance; third, baptism by immersion for the remission of sins; fourth, laying on of hands for the gift of the Holy Ghost.

5. We believe that a man must be called of God by prophecy, and by the laying on of hands by those who are in authority, to preach the Gospel and administer the ordinances thereof.

6. We believe in the same organization that existed in the primitive church, viz. apostles, prophets, pastors teachers, evangelists, etc.

7. We believe in the gift of tongues, prophecy, revelation, visions, healing, interpretation of tongues, etc.

8. We believe the Bible to be the word of God, as far as it is translated correctly; we also believe the Book of Mormon to be the word of God.

9. We believe all that God has revealed, all that He does now reveal, and we believe that he will yet reveal many great and important things pertaining to the Kingdom of God.

10. We believe in the literal gathering of Israel and in the restoration of the Ten Tribes. That Zion will be built upon this continent. That Christ will reign personally upon the earth, and that the earth will be renewed and receive its paradisaic glory.

11. We claim the privilege of worshipping Almighty God according to the dictates of our conscience, and allow all men the same privilege; let them worship how, where, or what they may.

12. We believe in being subject to kings, presidents, rulers and magistrates, in obeying, honoring and sustaining the law.

13. We believe in being honest, true, chaste, benevolent, virtuous, and in doing good to all men; indeed we may say that we follow the admonition of Paul, "We believe all things, we hope all things." We have endured many things, and hope to be able to endure all things. If there is anything virtuous, lovely or of good report, or praiseworthy, we seek after these things.

is prophecy put into practice. Smith dictated three new books of scripture for his followers: The Book of Mormon, The Doctrine and Covenants, and The Pearl of Great Price. The Mormon Church also uses the King James Bible, which is an English translation first published in 1610. Together, these four books are called "the standard works," meaning the standard or foundation of Mormon theology and doctrine.

The Book of Mormon is like the Bible in some ways. Each chapter, or "book," is the testimony of a prophet. The Book foretells the coming of Christ and His ministry, and tells of Christ's work with His disciples. However, the Book is very different from the Bible, too. The story takes place in ancient America, not the Middle East. And the ministry of Jesus occurs among ancient Americans. The Book came forth in America, all at once, complete, rather than collected in pieces over many centuries—as the Bible was.

The Doctrine and Covenants (1835) is a collection of 133 revelations given to Smith, plus five revelations received by his successors. These revelations were God's commandments and counsel given to Smith and the early Church.

The Pearl of Great Price (1830–1842) is a slim book of scripture with seven chapters and three pictures. The first picture is Smith's vision of Moses and the creation of the world. The second is Smith's "translation" of the Abraham story from an Egyptian papyrus. Also included is Smith's personal story (1838) and his Articles of Faith (1842).

The Joseph Smith Translation of the Bible (1830–1833) is another key Mormon scripture. Smith believed the King James Bible could be improved, so he edited a Mormon version, called the Joseph Smith Translation. He said in 1843, "There are many things in the Bible which do not, as they now stand, accord with the revelations of the Holy Ghost to me," (as quoted in *The Words of Joseph Smith: The Contemporary Accounts of the Nauvoo Discourses of the Prophet Joseph*).

Mormon Priesthood

The LDS Church has a lay priesthood where all men deemed worthy may be ordained. The priesthood is the authority to act in God's name. The Church teaches that God's authority cannot be assumed by someone who simply feels a sense of calling: One must be ordained by those who are in authority.

Mormons have two orders of priesthood—Melchizedek and Aaronic—which are based upon the priesthood in the Old Testament. The Melchizedek order oversees the spiritual aspects of the Church, while the Aaronic order oversees the temporal or material aspects of the Church. Within each order are offices or levels, found in both the New and Old Testaments.

The Melchizedek Priesthood is the greater of the two, named after Melchizedek, a great high priest mentioned in the Bible. The offices within it are elder, seventy, high priest, patriarch, apostle, and president of the high priesthood (prophet).

The Aaronic Priesthood is the lesser priesthood, named after the order of Aaron, the brother of Moses. The offices within it are deacon, teacher, priest, and bishop.

Women and the Mormon Priesthood

The LDS Church is led by an all-male priesthood. It does not ordain women to priesthood offices. However, women share in the priesthood with their husbands, and they perform women's priesthood rites in the temples.

Mormon women in the 19th century participated more in priesthood functions—such as blessings and healings—were ordained to offices, and presided over the women's Relief Society. These practices were restricted at the end of the 19th century, yet they still echo in today's LDS Church, especially in the Relief Society. The women's Relief Society is one of the largest women's organizations in the world, with 5 million members. It was established in 1842 as a female society or sisterhood. Today, the society offers instruction for women, handles much of the work in the wards and stakes (see page 18), gives compassionate service, aids and assists priesthood leaders and church members as well as nonmembers, and administers a literacy program in several countries.

Mormon Views of God and Human Beings

Mormons view God as an anthropomorphic being, which means they think of God as having a physical, human form. He has a glorified human body of flesh and bones. They believe all humans are created in the image of God. Unlike Christians, they do not believe God is a trinity (a three-in-one being made up of father, son, and holy spirit). For

Reminder of the past
In 2002, the LDS Church completed a major restoration of its temple in Nauvoo, Illinois, the first temple built by early members of the church before they left on their journey to Utah.

Mormons, God is three separate beings: God the Father, Jesus Christ, and the Holy Ghost. They are one in purpose but they are individual personages. God also has a wife, known as God the Mother.

In Mormon theology, God is both monotheistic (one God) and polytheistic (many gods). That is, there is one God who governs this planet and guides human salvation. However, there are many other planets in this vast universe and other beings in need of salvation. They too have Gods who are exalted human beings.

Mormons believe that human beings have a dual nature: spirit and body. The spirit is eternal and never dies, while the body is mortal and will die. God is the father of the spirit, but the physical body was formed from the elements of this planet. The spirit lived in heaven with God before coming down to earth and receiving a body.

Earth is a testing place where spirits prove worthy to return to God. When the body dies, the spirit returns to God and waits for res-urrection, which is the return to life of the dead; then the body will rise again and reunite with the spirit as an immortal being.

Smith taught that matter and spirit are connected. He taught that there is an intelligence within every spirit that is co-eternal with God and was not created by Him. This is the pure, divine part of the soul that guides the spirit and body toward redemption.

The Mormon view of salvation (achieving new life or being saved after death) relies upon both grace and works. Salvation comes through Jesus Christ and his atonement of suffering, death, and resurrection. It is available to all as redemption or resurrection into immortal life. This is the grace of God.

Yet the quality of one's salvation depends upon one's deeds in this life and one's knowledge of God or relationship with Him. Mormons believe that there are three kingdoms of heavenly salvation: telestial, terrestrial, and celestial. Salvation itself comes in two types: resurrection and exaltation. Those who are resurrected will inherit the telestial and terrestrial kingdoms of heaven. These beings are immortal. People who are exalted will inherit the celestial kingdom. These beings are resurrected and immortal and they become Gods, having spirit children and worlds of their own.

More than One Mormon Church

Most people are familiar with one LDS Church, which has its head-quarters in Salt Lake City, Utah. However, Joseph Smith's visions gave birth to two major churches, and dozens of smaller ones. Today, nearly 100 different churches or groups all trace their religious heritage to Joseph Smith's beginnings.

The Church of Jesus Christ of Latter-day Saints (LDS) in Salt Lake City is the major church in the Mormon tradition, with nearly 112 million members worldwide. The Church prefers to be called by its formal name rather than the nickname of Mormon. This church is the topic of this book.

The other main church in the Mormon tradition is the Community of Christ (RLDS), located in Independence, Missouri, which today has 250,000 members in 50 countries.

Sacred Mormon Rites

Similar to Christian sacraments, these sacred rites of the Mormon faith are performed by ordained members of the priesthood.

Baptism: A complete immersion under water symbolizes the cleansing of sins and baptizes one as a member of the church. Mormon children are baptized at the age of eight.

Blessings: A blessing is the laying on of hands accompanied by words of blessing. There are many types of blessings. A patriarchal blessing is a life overview given by a patriarch or elder of the church. A priesthood blessing is one given by a priesthood holder. Blessings are also given for those who are ill or in need, or by a father or mother.

Confirmation: After baptism, the laying on of hands for the gift of Holy Spirit confirms one as a member of the church.

Name and Blessing: This is a blessing prayer given to new babies, which includes bestowing their full name, upon which Mormons place great importance.

Ordination: In this rite, men are ordained to an office in the Aaronic or Melchizedek Priesthood, by the laying on of hands, performed by a man who holds proper priesthood authority. Setting Apart is a laying on of hands when any church member is called to serve in a lay church position.

Sacrament: Mormon communion is called the Sacrament and consists of broken pieces of bread and tiny paper cups of water. Priests bless the Sacrament with a special prayer and deacons serve it to the members. The bread and water symbolize the bread and wine served by Jesus as the last supper, his last meeting with his apostles before he was crucified (killed). For many Christians, the bread and wine also symbolize Christ's body and blood.

To attain the highest, the celestial kingdom, people must pass life's tests and receive all the ordinances, or blessings, of the Gospel—which are only obtained from the restored priesthood of the Church of Jesus Christ of Latter-day Saints.

Mormons do missionary work to give outsiders the blessings of salvation. They also do genealogy and temple rites for the dead (see page 77) to give departed spirits a chance to be ordained into the priesthood attained by all Mormon men before the final resurrection.

LDS Church Structure

The principal aim of the LDS Church, according to Church doctrine, is "the preparation of a people for the coming of the Lord; a people who will build the New Jerusalem." This is done through the "gathering of Israel" to the "Stakes of Zion."

A stake is named for the stake of a tent; together with other stakes, they anchor the "tent of Zion." The stakes are the basic building blocks of the structure of the Church, growing from small congregations or wards made up of 200 to 400 members. A branch is a prospective ward of 150 members or less, supervised by a branch president.

A stake is five to 10 wards with 2,000 to 4,000 members, supervised by a stake president and two counselors. A district is a prospective stake, supervised by a district president.

A stake is like a mini-version of the entire Church, and like the larger Church has a presidency of three people and a leadership council of 12. A mission is several stakes or districts, usually within one state or country. It is supervised by a mission president.

An area is a huge geographical region of the globe, containing several missions across states or countries, supervised by an area authority. The Church is the entire membership around the globe, including more than 160 countries; it is supervised by the general authorities.

Global administration of the Church is headed by the prophet/president and his two counselors. They and the Quorum of the Twelve Apostles, the top dozen leaders of the church, are all "prophets, seers and revelators" whom Mormons believe receive divine revelation to guide the church. They are also the principal policy-makers for the LDS Church.

In the LDS Church, leaders are called by God, meaning that higher leaders call lower leaders, after praying for guidance to know whom God wishes to choose.

Mormon Practices

In order to be an LDS Church member in good standing, one must follow the guidelines of the Church—keep the commandments, sustain the leaders, attend church meetings, behave morally, be honest with others, fulfill duties to family and church callings, pay a full tithing (a percentage of one's income) to the Church, and keep the "word of wisdom" (see page 21). If a member of the LDS Church does all these things, they are considered worthy to enter a Mormon temple and participate in sacred temple rites.

Sunday is the Sabbath, also known as the Lord's day of rest, for members of the LDS Church. Mormons meet together in a chapel every Sunday for three meetings, which last three hours in total. "Sacrament meeting" or "sacrament of the Lord's supper" is a communion of

Inside the temple
This photo shows one of the many types of rooms in an LDS temple. This is the Celestial Room of the temple in Boston, which opened in 2000.

sanctified bread and water served to the congregation. It is followed by two "talks" or sermons given by Church members, along with hymn singing.

Sunday school is an individual class for each age group. Relief Society and Priesthood meetings, and Young Men/Young Women, separate the men from the women and the boys from the girls for individual instruction. Several times a year, all the wards in the stake meet together for a stake conference. And once every six months, the Church holds a general conference in Salt Lake City that is broadcast to all stakes around the world.

Members of the Church practice the law of tithing as it was taught in the Old Testament. The word *tithe* means "tenth." Members donate a 10th of their income to the Church. The LDS Church is supported by the tithes and offerings of its members, which enables the church to finance buildings, education, welfare, missionary work, temples, curriculum, education, published materials in dozens of languages, global administration, humanitarian work and other programs that benefit Mormons and others worldwide.

Members also give "fast offerings" once a month to help the needy. Members fast (go without food) for two meals and donate the money they would have spent on those meals to Church programs. The church also owns a large number of commercial properties and investments, which contribute funds to Church projects, as well as to non-church communities and charities.

One Mormon scripture has become a well-known practice of Latter-day Saints. The "word of wisdom" is found in the Doctrine and Covenants, Section 89. This scripture counsels Mormons to take care of their health and avoid tobacco, alcohol, and "hot drinks" (except for medicinal purposes). It also suggests eating very little meat, but endorses eating grains, fruits, and vegetables. Thus Mormons do not drink coffee, tea, and alcohol; some Mormons also do not drink colas and other drinks that contain caffeine.

In addition, the Church urges moral standards of honesty and decency, as well as obedience to law (both secular, or civic, laws and Church laws). Members must abstain from sexual relations outside of marriage and be faithful within marriage. The Church opposes abortion, pornography, gambling, and immoral behavior (see chapters 4 and 5 for more on these positions).

If a Church member is found to be "contrary to the laws and order of the Church" they may be disciplined by a Church tribunal— either the bishop and his two counselors, or the stake president and his high council. A member may be placed on probation or "disfellowshipped," yet still remain a member. The most extreme judgement of the Church courts is excommunication, which severs a member permanently from the Church.

TEMPLE CEREMONIES

Mormons believe that these sacred rites performed in Mormon temples create eternal bonds that continue after death.

Dedication of Grave: A prayer of dedication given to a burial site by one who holds the priesthood.

Temple Endowment: A sacred ritual that conveys knowledge and power from God. It includes anointing and clothing Mormons with garments of the priesthood.

Second Endowment: the highest rite of the Mormon faith, also known as "calling and election made sure," signifying one's permanent connection to the Church.

Temple Sealing: A private, sacred ritual that "seals" or binds people together for eternity. Couples are sealed in eternal marriage, and children are sealed to parents.

Vicarious Ordinances: Rites performed on behalf of those who have died (see page 77).

From its beginnings in the 1820s, Mormons have been especially resourceful. This early Mormon character continues today in the Church and its members, who are regarded as resourceful and energetic. They work hard to launch new projects and goals, ever looking forward to new horizons and expansion. They value freedom, growth, productivity, prosperity, community, loyalty, and family.

Service in the Mormon Church

Men, women, and youth fill all the roles and positions in the wards and stakes, doing the work of the Church. Stakes and wards have no paid ministry; the labor required to run a stake or ward is carried out by the members themselves. Every willing member of the ward has ample opportunity to serve, share their talents and to learn new skills. Members fill administrative roles, teaching positions, or service-oriented roles, and work on a wide variety of social projects and events. If a

The Mormon Temple

The most prominent symbol of Mormon faith in American culture is the Salt Lake Temple with its massive granite walls and towers reaching to soaring heights with six-pointed, lighted spires. The gold statue of the angel Moroni stands atop the highest tower, 210 feet above the ground, and is shown playing a heraldic trumpet. The design of the Salt Lake Temple is based on the Nauvoo Temple, the first temple built by the early LDS Church members in Illinois (see page 29). Likewise, the Washington, D.C., Temple is patterned after the Salt Lake Temple, in a modernized form.

Today there are more than 100 LDS temples of in many styles around the world, including the reconstructed Nauvoo Temple in Illinois, completed in 2002.

The temple is a sanctuary, known as "the house of the Lord"—a sacred space where God or His spirit can dwell. It symbolizes the eternal or heavenly on earth.

All LDS temples provide a holy space for devoted Mormons to obtain heavenly blessings in temple rituals. Temple ceremonies convey the most sacred priesthood rites and bind relationships for eternity, sealing family members together forever. Mormons also perform baptism, confirmation, and sealing rites on behalf of their deceased ancestors (see the box on page 21).

Temples are not open to the general public and even many LDS people cannot enter. Only orthodox members who conform to LDS policies and requirements may receive a "temple recommend," which is permission to enter the temple. Temples divide the obedient from the casual Mormons.

member moves to a new city or country, they fit into the new ward easily because the Church structure, format, meetings, programs, and materials are the same all around the world.

Mormon boys and girls have their own organizations with unique programs and leadership roles. The Young Men's organization trains boys ages 12 to 17 to work, lead others, play sports, and acquire job and household skills.

The Young Women's organization trains girls, ages 12 to 17, to be organized, lead others, enjoy recreation, and learn job and household skills. Most of all, both organizations aim to help boys and girls to develop a personal relationship with God and to put that first in their lives. The Young Men and Young Women meet together every Sunday for classes with their own age group; they also meet several times during the month for social activities. During the school year, all high school youth in grades 9 through 12 attend daily "seminary" classes to study LDS Church history, scriptures, doctrine, and theology.

TEMPLE SQUARE
The worldwide headquarters of the LDS Church is Temple Square in Salt Lake City, Utah. From this location, LDS Church leaders manage the 11-million-member global faith. Occupying one full city block, the square is the focal point of the city and includes the Salt Lake Temple, the dome-shaped Mormon Tabernacle, Assembly Hall, and two visitor's centers. Adjacent to the Square are the Family History Library and the Church Museum, the Relief Society Building, the Joseph Smith Memorial, the Church Office Building, the Lion House, Beehive House, the Church Administration Building, and the new LDS Conference Center.

The First American Religion Is Born

JOSEPH SMITH'S VISIONS INSPIRED HUNDREDS OF PEOPLE TO FOLLOW him in the early days. They soon began a decades-long search for a home, for a place where Mormons could freely practice what they believed. It would be a bumpy road, filled with controversy and tragedy. Less than two decades after Smith's first meeting with the angels, he would be dead, but the church he founded would finally be in a place where it could live.

First Encounters

In 1820, the 15-year-old Smith saw two personages whom he later identified as Jesus and God the Father. Their message was simple: Smith should not join any of the existing churches that were competing for his attention. They were all wrong. As noted in the introduction, the area of western New York in which young Smith lived was contested space where evangelists spent the summer months stirring the fires of revival and seeking members from among the large number of people who did not attend church. So often were revival meetings held that the region became known as the "burned-over-district," after the fiery speeches made by the roving preachers.

Three years later, Smith, now 18, was visited by an angel named Moroni. Moroni told Smith about a set of ancient gold plates that were buried

Joseph Smith, Jr.
This portrait of the LDS Church founder was painted by Sutcliffe Maudsley in 1842.

on a hill (today a sacred site for Mormons called Cumorah) near his home, and of the existence of two stones (called Thurim and Umim) which would facilitate his translation of the texts he would find on the plates. The texts were written in what Smith described as "reformed Egyptian." Eventually the exact location of the plates was disclosed to Smith and he was allowed to dig them up. He spent two years working on the translation, which was published in 1830 as the Book of Mormon.

From the beginning, Smith and his new revelation stirred a storm of controversy. Some of the book's first reviewers (the first of a line of reviewers that stretches to the present) questioned its accuracy and

The Founder Recounts Meeting God

Joseph Smith is quoted in *A History of the Church* (published in 1902) describing his encounter with Jesus and God the Father in this way:

> *After I had retired to the place where I had previously designed to go, having looked around me, and finding myself alone, I kneeled down and began to offer up the desires of my heart to God. I had scarcely done so, when immediately I was seized upon by some power which entirely overcame me, and had such an astonishing influence over me as to bind my tongue so that I could not speak. Thick darkness gathered around me, and it seemed to me for a time as if I were doomed to sudden destruction.*
>
> *But, exerting all my powers to call upon God to deliver me out of the power of this enemy which had seized upon me, and at the very moment when I was ready to sink into despair and abandon myself to destruction—not to an imaginary ruin, but to the power of some actual being from the unseen world, who had such marvelous power as I had never before felt in any being—just at this moment of great alarm, I saw a pillar of light exactly over my head, above the brightness of the sun, which descended gradually until it fell upon me.*
>
> *It no sooner appeared than I found myself delivered from the enemy which held me bound. When the light rested upon me I saw two Personages, whose brightness and glory defy all description, standing above me in the air. One of them spake unto me, calling me by name and said, pointing to the other—This is My Beloved Son. Hear Him!*

authenticity. However, despite its rejection by many, others found in it truths that spoke to them, and they began to flock around Smith and the Church of Jesus Christ he founded in 1830.

From the book they learned the story of the first Americans, the Native peoples. According to the book, America was first populated by a group of Israelites, the Jeredites, who migrated from the Middle East at the time the Tower of Babel was built (recounted in the Bible in Genesis, chapter 11), and a second group who left Palestine following the destruction of Jerusalem. Native Americans were the remnant of the second group, which had been all but destroyed in the fourth century. The Book of Mormon is an historical account of these American Israelites written down by the last of their prophet-leaders.

From Smith and several close associates, people learned of the reestablishment of the "true Church," symbolized by the reintroduction of the priesthood in two orders: The priesthood of Aaron, to which all males were accepted, and a higher priesthood of Melchizedek, an order for those who assume a post in the Church, from the young men sent out on missions to the apostles who lead the Church.

Smith gathered a small circle of early believers around him and from among them came the future leaders of the church. Their leadership skills would be tested sooner than any of them thought.

On to Ohio

Very soon after the Church was formed, Smith moved to Kirtland, Ohio, in the northeast corner of that state. The majority of Church members gathered there, many buying land for what they assumed would be a permanent settlement. However, neighbors reacted negatively to both Smith and the Church, and in 1832 showed their displeasure by tarring and feathering him. Not dissuaded, Smith recovered from his ordeal and led in the building of the first Mormon temple. Able to survive in the face of hostile neighbors, the new community was dealt a harsh blow by a general financial collapse in 1837. In January 1838, they left Kirtland as a group for what they hoped to be a better life in Missouri.

Their new home did not provide the hoped-for peace and stability, and within a few months even the governor of the state had turned against Smith and his followers. By the end of the year they were on the move again, forced out of another home again by people by who did not agree with their beliefs. Arrested for treason, Smith escaped by bribing a guard and was able to join his fellow Church members in Illinois. There, beside the slow-moving Mississippi River, the Mormons appeared to have found their haven. Under Smith's guidance they built a new city, which they called Nauvoo the Beautiful. On the hill overlooking the town and river, they erected a new temple. Within a few years, Nauvoo was the largest city in Illinois.

Members of the Church of Jesus Christ of Latter-day Saints saw themselves as the members of a restored Christian Church, a church that had ceased to exist with the passing of Jesus' original apostles.

The first temple

This Mormon temple in Kirtland, Ohio, was built and dedicated in 1836 by the early members of the LDS Church. This photo shows the temple in the early 1900s.

That the Church had been reestablished was also a sign that the last days were upon humanity. With the Mormons thus looking for the imminent return of their Lord, they were spurred even more enthusiastically to find a place to gather for His appearance.

While sharing many beliefs with other Christians, the Mormons held to several ideas that separated them from their Christian neighbors. First was the matter of the new revelation. Not only had Smith translated the Book of Mormon, but he became the source of additional revelations. He translated two additional books, the Book of Moses and the Book of Abraham. He also regularly received revelations for the ongoing guidance of the Church. These were first gathered in 1833 as the Book of Commandments. Future editions, containing later revelations, were published as the Doctrine and Covenants. Smith also began, but did not complete, a new edition of the Bible with material added that he had received by revelation. Most Christians do not accept the Book of Mormon or these additional texts, which are held sacred by Mormons.

Smith published a set of beliefs to which adherents of his church subscribed, but most Christians took great offense at what he proposed. Christians commonly believe in the doctrine of the Trinity, the idea that the one God exists in three persons: God the Father, Jesus His Son and the Holy Spirit. Smith, instead, proposed the existence of three distinct divine personages. Smith also denied several traditional Christian beliefs such as original sin (the concept that all people are born sinners because Adam and Eve disobeyed God), while affirming continuing revelation and the idea that America, not the Holy Land in the Middle East, would be the site of the New Jerusalem to come. Other Christian beliefs not included in the Mormon Articles of Faith (see page 13) served to further distance the Church from traditional Christian believers. The difficulties that the LDS Church had with other Christians were among the reasons the group had such a hard time finding a home they could call their own. It was not a time in America of great tolerance of beliefs that were outside the mainstream.

Problems at Nauvoo

The Mormons prospered at Nauvoo. Among the many residents in the carefully laid out city, one could find, for example, Jonathan Browning (see page 99), whose gun shop would be the beginning of the famous Browning Arms Company. There were a wide variety of industries,

LAST DAYS

The Biblical book of Revelation describes what the end of the world will be like. These "last days," says Revelation, will be foretold by many signs and will involve a violent clash between the forces of good and evil. Some Christians believe that the last days are coming soon.

from blacksmithing to publishing. Smith organized an armed militia, the Nauvoo Legion, and took an active role in state and even national politics. He launched a campaign for the American presidency in 1844.

Smith's involvement in politics may have been the key to the disaster that struck the community in 1844. The zealous Mormons tended to share the same political views, and in a state that was otherwise evenly divided between the two major political parties, the Mormons voting as a block could easily sway elections. When Smith suggested he might use this block of votes at Nauvoo as a bargaining chip in Illinois state politics, many were angry at the Mormons. Others looked jealously at Mormon economic success, especially in the nearby county seat, Carthage, and in the nearby river port city of Warsaw.

A Tragic End

The immediate problem leading to the Mormon downfall at Nauvoo was the departure from church membership of three men: William Law, Charles Foster, and C. L. Higbee. With their friends, they established a rival church in the heart of Nauvoo, and Law launched a newspaper that, he claimed, would voice their opinions about Smith and the church he lead. All three men also began legal actions against Smith on charges that ranged from adultery to slander.

Events came to a head in June, 1844. The first issue of Law's paper, the *Nauvoo Expositer*, appeared on June 7. Smith declared the paper a public nuisance and the Nauvoo Legion, Smith's armed militia, destroyed the newspaper's offices. Statewide public anger at Smith reached new heights, while newspapers in Warsaw and Carthage called for the elimination of the Mormons. Smith left for a short stay in Iowa, but soon returned.

Smith allowed himself to be arrested on the unusual charge of treason, based on the technicality that he had declared martial law in Nauvoo. He was jailed in Carthage and guarded by a small group of militia drawn from the Carthage area.

Several days after Smith was jailed, along with his brother Hyrum (1800–1844) and two of the Church's Apostles—John Taylor (1808–1887) and Willard Richards (1804–1854)—a mob stormed the jail and began shooting. When the smoke cleared, Joseph and Hyrum Smith were dead. Taylor had taken five bullets but later recovered. Richards escaped without being shot. The first era of the Church of Jesus Christ of Latter-day Saints had come to an abrupt and violent end.

After the Prophet's Death

The sudden death of the prophet left the Mormons in chaos and the Church leaderless. Several people stepped forward to assume Smith's role. Among the first was Sidney Rigdon (1801–1877), organizationally next in line but out of favor with Church leadership. Jesse James Strange (1813–1856), a leader from Wisconsin who had begun to receive revelations, was also rejected. In the end, Brigham Young (1801–1877,

A violent death
While under arrest in Nauvoo, Joseph Smith and his brother Hyrum were murdered in 1844, as shown in this 1976 painting by Gary Smith.

see page 41), one of the Church's Apostles, who at the time of Smith's death had been in England on a mission, eventually returned to Nauvoo, rallied the deflated Mormons, and became the Church's next prophet and president.

Young was aware that the Church's days in Nauvoo were numbered and, with Church leaders, began to create a plan to move West, beyond the reach of the United States government. In the meantime, Church members hurried to complete the temple so it could be used for the first set of the special services for which it was designed. However, in September 1845, more anti-Mormon violence occurred and in the spring of 1846 Young began to make the planned move public. The temple was finished and dedicated in December 1846 and more than 6,000 Church members participated in their private ceremonies over the next few months.

The migration began in February 1847 and by September several thousand former Nauvoo residents had found their way to Winter Quarters (now Florence), Nebraska, where a temporary village had been hastily constructed. Eventually some 4,000 people made their way to Winter Quarters, where they expected to pause before heading West. During the winter of 1846–47, food was short and some 600 people died.

Young left as soon as weather allowed early in 1847, and laid out a trail to the Salt Lake Valley in what is today Utah. Soon afterward the surviving Church members began their trek.

Other Churches Emerge

Not everyone made the move to Utah. Among those who stayed were Smith's widow, Emma, and her son, Joseph Smith III. Over the next decade, those members of the Mormon Church who did not move to Utah organized separately. One small group moved to Independence, Missouri, and purchased the land that had been designated as the site of a new temple, and organized an independent Church of Christ.

The largest number of those who did not make the trek West, however, eventually came together in 1860 to form the Reorganized Church of Jesus Christ of Latter Day Saints (note the capital D in Day; the Mormons who made their home in Salt Lake City spell their church's name with a hyphen and a lowercase d in day). They chose Joseph Smith III to lead them. They had become particularly disturbed by Young's announcement in 1852 that members in Utah had adopted

First home out West
This 1865 painting by C.C.A. Christensen shows the log cabins built at Winter Quarters, where Mormon pioneers spent the winter of 1846–1847 while heading West to find a new place to practice their faith.

polygamy (having several wives at the same time) as a Church practice. The Reorganized Church saw itself as continuing the church as it existed under Joseph Smith, Jr., and staunchly opposed polygamy and other doctrines they claimed were being introduced by Young. Although Smith himself married 27 women, Young made it a more prominent part of Mormon doctrine.

"This Is the Place"

Young had to find his Church a home. He left Winter Quarters on April 5, 1847, with an advance group (143 men, three women, and two children). Young became ill during the journey and fell behind as the main group moved ahead. He finally arrived at the Salt Lake Valley on July 24. It is noted that immediately upon seeing it stretched out before him, he announced, "This is the place."

Over the next month, he directed the exploration of the northern part of the valley (the present site of Salt Lake City), assisted with the initial surveys, and designated the spot for a new temple. Then on August 26, he left the valley to return to Winter Quarters to assist with the process of migration. Young's actions gave clear evidence of the organizational skills he would further demonstrate as Church members settled across Utah and neighboring states.

2

Key Events in Mormon History

WITH THEIR PROMISED LAND IN SIGHT, THE LDS CHURCH RAPIDLY began a process of settlement that would ultimately spread their influence—spiritually, politically, and culturally—throughout Utah and bordering territories and states. For the rest of the 19th century, a series of events, from within and from outside the Mormon community, had a large impact on how this influence spread.

As the 20th century began, the Mormon community was battling prejudices and attitudes that, by the end of that century, had largely disappeared. The story of that journey is a big part of the history of the American West.

Settling a City

Within hours after Brigham Young declared that the wandering Mormons had found their home, the industrious pioneers had begun tilling the soil and planting crops. The day Young arrived, July 24, has since been immortalized in annual Pioneer Day celebrations (see page 81). Shelters were quickly erected and a camp for the nearly 150 first arrivals was also set up.

A few days later, plans began to be drawn up to create Great Salt Lake City. (To the northwest of the Mormon encampment was Salt Lake, an inland sea that is the largest and saltiest body of water west of the Mississippi River.)

PRECEDING PAGE
A great leader
More than any other person, Brigham Young formed the organization that is today the Church of Jesus Christ of Latter-day Saints. Under his leadership, the Church moved to Utah and established its international headquarters in Salt Lake City.

The city Young formed was laid out in a grid pattern of 10-acre squares. Visitors today often are surprised by its many wide boulevards that still define the city. These streets were created in those first years to be 132 feet wide, a distance that left enough room for a team of four oxen and a wagon to make a U-turn.

For the Mormons, who had been almost literally chased out of every other settlement they had attempted to establish, this pristine wilderness was a promised land. Here, they felt, they could set up a city and create lives that mirrored their beliefs, as part of a community of fellow believers. To that end, a city council was set up by the end of the year 1847 and a set of city ordinances was put in place on January 1, 1848.

The settlement was still fairly small at that point, but more immigrants were trickling in. It was the long, harsh winter of 1847–48, and the Mormons battled drought and frost. The provident arrival of a flock of seagulls (see the box at left) was seen by the faithful as, literally, a Godsend.

Thanks to a gold rush in California (see page 39), Salt Lake City (the word *Great* was dropped in 1862) grew rapidly. However, many of the new arrivals were not Mormons and Young saw a threat to Mormon control of the city and the region. In 1849, he formed the Perpetual Emigrating Company to create a fund that would help more Mormons from America and Europe find their way to his new city. In addition, Mormons from Salt Lake City fanned out around the area, establishing future Utah cities including Provo and Ogden, as well as founding settlements in California and the New Mexico territory. With these settlers came Mormon ways and Mormon industriousness; they worked as hard at winning new converts as they did at building their settlements.

Young called the overall sweep of lands claimed by Mormons the State of Deseret. The word means honeybee and stands for the hardworking character of Mormons. Today, Utah is known as the Beehive State and a beehive is on the state seal.

The federal government rejected the name Deseret in 1850 and created the Utah Territory, naming the area after the resident Native Americans, the Utes. Salt Lake City itself was officially incorporated in 1851 and became the permanent capital of the territory in 1856.

Gold!

Mormon settlers were dramatically affected by the discovery of gold in northern California in January, 1848. The gold rush that ensued over the next few years drew thousands of prospectors to the West, and Salt Lake City became a key stopover for men on the way to the gold fields. The city grew dramatically in size, and local merchants profited by selling mining supplies and other items needed by gold prospectors.

The new arrivals were a great benefit to the young city, but at the same time, their mostly non-Mormon character tested the cohe-

Walking in their footsteps
In 1997, hundreds of LDS Church members recreated the pioneer journey of their ancestors from Illinois to Utah. Using wagons and handcarts similar to those used by the original settlers, they relived the paths of the past.

sion and faith of the Latter-day Saints' community. Once again, in a pattern that would be repeated in decades to come, the outside world was making life difficult for a community that wanted to live its own life its own way.

While the gold rush itself is a widely- known historical fact, most readers would be surprised to learn that Mormons were also deeply involved in the discovery of gold itself. In January of 1848, James Marshall (1810–1885) brought a handful of gold dust to the office of John Sutter (1803–1880). Sutter was a Mormon and owner of the sawmill where Marshall had been working when he discovered the gold. Sutter used chemicals and scales to determine that the substance was indeed gold, and later went with Marshall to see the site in person.

Soon after, another Mormon, Samuel Brannan, who owned a general store in the area, heard of the find. As Sutter wrote in a November 1857 article in *Hutchings' California Magazine*, "[Brannan] sent up large supplies of goods, leased a larger house from me and commenced a very large and profitable business; soon he opened a branch house of business at Mormon Island." That site, named for the settlers of the region (including Sutter), was one of the main prospecting sites in the early gold rush days. Sutter also wrote that Mormon settlers who worked for him soon "got gold fever like everybody else, and after they made their piles [of money] they left for the Great Salt Lake."

Brannan later was one of the key people to spread the news of the gold strike. He supposedly went to San Francisco, then the largest city in the West, and walked the streets brandishing gold dust and telling his tale of the strike. Of course, he was trying to drum up business for his stores, and it worked. The gold rush was on; within a year, California was so crowded with people that it quickly became a state of the United States. For the Mormon settlers in Salt Lake City and other Utah towns, it was a decidedly mixed blessing, because it turned the eyes of the nation, and the federal government, to the West.

The Utah War

About a decade after Young led the Mormon pioneers into the Salt Lake Valley, they faced the greatest challenge to their independence. The gold rush had drawn thousands of new settlers, and they sent back East details of the Mormon's non-traditional beliefs and practices. In Wash-

Brigham Young

After Joseph Smith, by far the most important and influential person in LDS history is Brigham Young, the man who brought the Mormons to the West. His influence on the LDS Church politically, spiritually, economically, and philosophically still resonates to today.

Young was born in Vermont. His family moved to upstate New York when he was very young. He grew up to be a skilled carpenter and builder. He was 29 years old when Joseph Smith's brother Samuel passed through Mendon, New York, where Young was living, and left a copy of the Book of Mormon. Young was impressed with the book, but did not convert immediately. In fact, he was not baptized into the LDS Church until 1832. His official biography on the Brigham Young University web site (www.byu.edu) reports that he was preaching sermons within a week, quoting him as saying at the time, "Nothing would satisfy me but to cry abroad in the world, what the Lord was doing in latter days." Young soon traveled to Kirtland, Ohio (see page 28), and met Joseph Smith.

In 1835, Young became one of the original Quorum of the Twelve Apostles (see page 19), the Church's senior leadership. He became a key missionary, leading an early trip to England to convert new members. He and the other Mormons then embarked on the numerous forced migrations described in chapter 1. Young became president of the church upon Smith's death in 1844; he remained president until his death 33 years later.

With the situation in Nauvoo (see chapter 1) deteriorating, Young decided to move West again and led 150 settlers into the Salt Lake Valley in 1847. Young then proceeded to direct nearly every aspect of the LDS community's life for three decades. He was the territorial governor. He married 27 women and had 56 children, thus supporting the continuing practice of polygamy that would prove to be so divisive in later years. He founded the college that would eventually bear his name—Brigham Young University. Young died in 1877 of a ruptured appendix.

In matters of faith, and matters of politics, and economics, Young's impact was monumental. Without his early leadership, there is little doubt that the LDS Church could never have become the regional power, and internationally growing religion, that it is today.

Early days
This 1865 photograph shows a street scene from a young Salt Lake City. Founded by LDS members and bolstered by the 1849 gold rush, the bustling city was, by this time, the capital of the future state of Utah.

ington, D.C., President James Buchanan, elected in 1856, felt that Young, then governor of the Utah Territory, posed a threat to federal control. A variety of small disagreements (including a dispute between Young and federally-appointed Justice W.W. Drummond of the Utah Territory Supreme Court) were blown somewhat out of proportion and Buchanan declared the Mormons to be in open revolt against the government.

Buchanan dispatched a large U.S. Army detachment to Utah in 1857 to remove Young from office and install Alfred Cumming as the new governor. The problem was that no one told Young of these moves, and as the army moved toward Utah, Young reacted strongly. Seeing yet another attempt by outside forces to remove Mormons from their land, he organized a force of men to counter the oncoming troops. The Utah War had begun.

However, it was a war with few skirmishes and no pitched battles. Winter intervened, and while the army troops froze in their camps

The Mountain Meadows Massacre

As U.S. Army troops were heading West in 1857 to install a new governor in Utah, non-Mormon settlers were also heading into the Utah Territory. Suspicion of outsiders ran high in the tense times, and that suspicion boiled over on September 11, 1857, to create one of the darkest days in Mormon history.

One of the non-Mormon wagon trains crossing southern Utah was attacked by Native Americans of the Piede tribe; more than 100 people were killed. It soon became clear that the Piede had been goaded to attack the pioneers by Mormons in the area. Although the Mormons' exact role in the massacre remains somewhat murky, most experts now believe that at least some Mormons were responsible for some of the murders.

The first complete look at the events of that day and those leading up to it was published in a 1950 book, *The Mountain Meadows Massacre*, by Juanita Brooks. Several more recent books have taken up the search for answers, as well. Brooks and later authors believe Brigham Young himself did not know of or orchestrate the massacre, but that he may have assisted in some of the cover-up actions taken by the LDS Church afterward.

Whatever actually happened, and this space does not allow for a full telling of the entire controversy, the Mountain Meadows Massacre is one of the most-debated events in Mormon history. With few real witnesses and many conflicting statements and motives, what truly happened there remains mostly conjecture. What was important at the time is that the tragedy reinforced the resolve of the federal government to remove the Mormons from power in the Utah Territory.

(harassed by Mormon soldiers throughout the cold months), negotiations were under way between Young and government representatives. As the talks continued, news of a terrible event reached Salt Lake City and changed Buchanan's view. The Mountain Meadows Massacre (see the box on page 43) and the resulting controversy steeled the federal government's resolve to break the Mormons' hold on the territory and put Young in a difficult place. Young and his fellow Mormons put together a plan called Move South, in which they would leave the city en masse, burning it as they went, to leave nothing for any "invading" army.

That plan never had to be enacted, however, because federal negotiators arranged for Cumming to enter the city unmolested as both Young and the federal troops stood down. On April 6, 1858, the matter was finally settled peacefully, with full recognition by Young of

Handcarts on the Trail

In the years before and after the Utah War, Mormon settlers continued to stream into Utah. But horses and wagons, the traditional mode of transportation, were expensive. Horses had to be fed and watered on the trail, and wagons broke down easily. Many of the Mormons used as transport a unique handcart that came to symbolize their determination to make the journey no matter what.

The handcarts were a thrifty and sturdy alternative. Modeled after carts used by street sweepers in large cities, the wooden handcarts weighed about 60 pounds and had two large wheels, like a wheelbarrow. They were 6 to 7 feet long and held about 500 pounds of gear in a tray-like box atop a single axle. A horizontal handle across the front of the cart let one or two people pull the cart as they walked along the trail.

Several large groups, or companies, of handcarts, made their way West in the late 1850s. In 1860, settlers from Salt Lake began using a type of oxen to pull wagons to the Midwest and pick up pioneers and carry them West, and the use of the handcarts died out.

Cumming's post as governor and a full pardon granted to all Mormon soldiers in the brief, but important conflict.

The Utah War essentially ended for good the Mormons' dream of a true nation of their own. As Harold Schindler wrote in a July 23, 1995, article in the *Salt Lake Tribune*, the Utah War "forever cracked their shell of isolationism."

One postscript to the war was that when the federal troops left, heading back to what would become the Civil War, they left behind millions of dollars worth of gear and supplies. The businesslike Mormons in the city quickly purchased the materials at a very low cost. It did not make up for the trauma of the end of sovereignty, but it helped.

The Railroad Arrives

Until 1869, Young and the Mormons depended on horsepower, ox power, and foot power (see the box on page 44) to bring its LDS Church members from the eastern United States to the newly settled lands of Deseret and the West. Thousands of Mormon pioneers walked thousands of miles, often literally carrying their worldly possessions on their backs. But in 1869, an event took place that had a massive impact on all the Western states and radically changed the world of the LDS Church in Utah.

On May 10, 1869, at Promontory Point, Utah, a golden spike was driven into a railbed, officially linking the continental United States with continuous rail service for the first time. The completion of the transcontinental railroad, a joint project of the Union Pacific and Central Pacific Railroads, had consumed the attention of a nation for a decade.

Its construction also affected the Mormon community. Railroad builders had appealed to Young for workers to help with the back-breaking labor needed to blast a railroad through forbidding mountains and prairies. Young was promised a large sum of money (some say more than $1 million) for the work of his community members, but as the last spike was driven in 1869, much of that money was still unpaid—and would, in fact, remain a sore subject for a long time.

The railroad, however, proved to be a mixed blessing for Young's community. While the ease of transport on the "iron horse" did mean that thousands more Mormons from other states could come to Utah, it also meant that many non-Mormons could find their way to Deseret.

Towns and cities that had been founded and almost entirely populated by Mormons had to deal with new citizens who did not always share their values and practices.

The railroad brought prosperity, commerce, and customers for Mormon businesses. However, like the gold rush 20 years earlier, it also brought influences that LDS leaders would spend decades battling against—influences that included alcohol, gambling, and prostitution.

The railroad was a double-edged sword, further opening up the sheltered world of the Mormons to pressure from the outside. However, it can also be argued that by opening up the country to their missionaries and community members, the railroad helped spread the Mormon faith farther and faster than handcarts and horses could have ever done.

The 1890 Manifesto and National Political Power

The issue of polygamy (one man having several wives) became the focus of nearly all interactions between the LDS Church and the federal government for most of the 19th century. That conflict will be covered in detail in chapter 4, but a key moment should be mentioned here.

In 1890, LDS president Wilford Woodruff (1807–1898) issued a new revelation that declared that the practice of plural marriage (polygamy) would no longer be a part of the practice of Mormonism. While polygamy continued unofficially for years, the official ban made dealing with the federal government much easier because polygamy was illegal in the United States.

In 1894, President Grover Cleveland issued an amnesty for men who had taken multiple wives, and in 1896 Utah became a state of the United States.

The removal of the polygamy policy enabled Utah to elect the first Mormon U.S. senator. Reed Smoot (1861–1941) was elected in 1902, but was not seated until 1907 because anti-Mormon forces tried to keep him out of the Senate. He remained in the Senate until 1932. Among his achievements was the landmark Smoot-Hawley Tariff Act, which restructured how the United States charges tariffs, or taxes, on international goods.

It is not too much of a reach to say that Smoot would not have been able to write that law had not Woodruff released the LDS Church from the constricting policy of polygamy. Further discussion of the polygamy issue can be found in chapters 4 and 5.

The Impact of David McKay

The election of David O. McKay (1873–1970) as president and prophet in 1951 was one of the most significant events in Mormon history. Before he ascended to the top post, he had been a part of the leadership as a member of the Quorum of the Twelve Apostles since 1906, and had been a counselor since 1934. He also was a leader in the LDS Church's education efforts.

In the 1920s, McKay spent several years abroad, traveling to the LDS's young international missions. From 1922 to 1924 he was the head of its European mission. In that position, he encouraged European Mormons to remain in their home countries rather than emigrate to Utah and other American LDS strongholds. This was a major change in the general policy of the LDS Church and many credit this with kickstarting the Church's worldwide expansion.

When he was elected to the presidency in 1951, he continued to focus on expansion. Under his tenure, membership tripled to nearly 3 million members worldwide. Temples were built in Britain, New

Spreading the faith
Latter-day Saints president and prophet David McKay led the LDS Church into a new era of worldwide expansion that saw membership nearly double during his tenure.

Zealand, and Switzerland, while organizational units were created in a dozen more countries. One of the sayings for which he was best-known is, "Every member a missionary," emphasizing the continuing efforts to expand the Church's membership.

He had an impact outside the Church as well, taking a firm stand against racism during the turbulent 1960s and encouraging LDS members to work for civil rights.

McKay's methods and ideas, as well as the expansion in sheer numbers of the Mormon population in the United States, meant those members began having more of an impact on political issues. The traditional Mormon values of family, faith, and community resounded in themes espoused by conservative Republicans, especially as shown in the 1980 election of President Ronald Reagan. Mormon values were seen as much more mainstream and popular than they had been viewed only a century earlier.

As will be shown in chapter 5, Mormon political power at the national level continued to expand in the last part of the 20th century. A key moment in that process arrived in November, 2002, when Mitt Romney (b.1947) was elected governor of Massachusetts. Romney is a practicing Mormon, a former bishop of the Massachusetts Mormon congregations, and only the second non-Protestant, non-Catholic governor of Massachusetts.

"A Mormon has won the governorship in Massachusetts," wrote Michael Paulson in the *Boston Globe* on September 9, 2002, "a development remarkable as much for how little controversy it occasioned as for happening at all. The election of Mitt Romney . . . demonstrates an increasing acceptance of Mormons in the United States, as well the increasing willingness of Americans to elect members of minority faiths."

A Rapidly Expanding Membership

The LDS Church continues to place vital importance on missionary work, and its fastest-growing membership bases are not in the United States, but in South American countries. As many as half of all Church members worldwide lived outside the United States in 2002—the first time that has been true in LDS history.

In the past 20 years, worldwide membership has nearly doubled— an amazing growth rate for a religion that, at the time of Brigham Young not too long ago, was little more than a tiny fraction of the American population. The journey from one man's vision to another man's dogged pursuit of that vision to the worldwide acceptance that vision enjoys today is one of the most remarkable in the history of worldwide religion. It is a story that continues to play itself out in all areas of American life.

3

Mormons and American Culture

DURING THE PERIOD BETWEEN THE REVOLUTION AND THE CIVIL War (c.1800–1860), Americans were laying the foundations for a uniquely American civilization and culture—developing native styles of literature, art, architecture, schools, law, politics, and more, as well as American forms of religion. In 1831, French philosopher Alexis de Tocqueville (1805–1895) wrote in *Democracy in America* that the United States had developed "a unique civilization, that was bound to influence the whole Western world."

Mormon culture emerged at the same time as American culture. Like America, Mormonism was brand new, with a new identity. Mormon culture was created from several elements: a theology that placed God's kingdom in human society; Yankee ingenuity, self-sufficiency, and pioneer homesteading; America's Western frontier; a gathering of immigrants from the eastern United States and Europe; and a cooperative society in which heart and mind were inseparable.

Mormons and Manifest Destiny

In the 1840s, Americans were possessed by the spirit of manifest destiny, a belief that the United States had the right and duty to extend itself all the way to the Pacific Coast. This was accomplished by letting Americans establish homes, farms and ranches in western regions (including the Indian and Mexican Territories, California, and Oregon). The Mormons embraced and affected manifest destiny on a larger scale than any other single group of Americans. It enabled the Mormons to leave what was then the United States and find a home—the Zion they had been seeking for 17 years.

Like other Americans, the Mormons moved West, but they went as one entire society transplanting itself and hoping to claim an entire region—the Great Basin stretching from the Rocky Mountains to the Sierra Mountains in California (490,000 square miles, four future states). The Mormons thought that in this Mexican-held territory, with its spacious, unsettled lands, they could establish their own society and government. And they felt they deserved it because they had helped the United States in the Mexican War (1846–1848, see the box on page 53).

The Mormons were granted about half the area they wanted (Utah, Nevada, parts of Colorado and Wyoming), an area called the Utah Territory after the native Ute people. Yet the Mormons spread out far beyond, establishing settlements in California, Idaho, Wyoming, Arizona, Colorado, New Mexico, Canada, and Mexico. By planting new towns across the entire western region, the Mormons helped bring the culture of the Western world to the American desert, greatly aiding establishment of the western United States and the fulfillment of manifest destiny.

In the West, Salt Lake City was a refuge and a permanent home for the Mormons, where they were able to really establish their identity. For the first time, the Mormon community was stable and settled. The settlements at Kirtland and Nauvoo (see pages 28–30) launched Mormonism as a new religious society and culture, but Salt Lake City stabilized it, creating an identity.

Moving West was essential for the Mormon faith to pursue its vision of Zion on earth and, in the process, find itself. In this process of leaving the United States and homesteading the western wilderness, Mormonism was, in the words of historian Harold Bloom in *The American Religion* (1992), "a religion that became a people." Only by leaving eastern society and moving into ungoverned lands could Mormons find enough freedom to live according to their ideals. On the western frontier, religious freedom and new communities were the way of life.

The Pioneer Experience

The dominant theme of 19th-century America was the great American westward migration, and the Mormons were a big part of that chapter in American history. The first half of the great American westward movement spread out from New England and Appalachia to the Mississippi River and its western shore states.

The second half, beginning in the 1840s, found pioneers heading west from the Mississippi and Missouri Rivers across the Great Plains to Texas, Oregon, California, and the Southwest. Major routes west opened up when the Oregon Territory was acquired in 1815. The Mormons joined in these two American westward movements and were a major force in both.

The western pioneer period of overland travel began about 1841 and ended in 1869 when the transcontinental railroad was finished. People still moved West after 1869, but they could ride on the railroad. Of the more than 600,000 overlanders who crossed the American plains between 1841 and 1869, about 70,000 were Mormons. These travelers overcame obstacles such as lack of supplies, rough terrain, and the attacks of both Native Americans and wild animals to reach their destination. New, incoming pioneers relied upon fellow Mormons in Salt Lake City for money, aid, and assistance.

During their first three years on the way West, from 1847 to 1849, the Mormon pioneers nearly starved to death, battling bad weather and insects for their crops, competing with wolves and Native Americans for animals and cattle. Some left to go back East or to California, lured by the gold rush in San Francisco. In 1849, travelers bound for the gold rush in California helped save the struggling Salt Lake City community by trading items with the Mormons.

Immediately upon their arrival in the Salt Lake Valley, members of the LDS Church were assigned by Brigham Young to set up new communities throughout the West. In all, the pioneers settled 600 communities in a broad swath stretching 1,350 miles from southern Alberta, Canada, into Mexico. These settlers laid out streets, planted crops, dug wells, irrigated land, built homes, and created societies based on their religion. Every family was motivated to build an inheritance for the community.

MORMONS IN THE MEXICAN WAR

In 1847, as the United States waged a territorial war with Mexico, a brigade of 500 Mormons was formed in Iowa to join the fighting. They marched to southern California to join regular U.S. Army troops near San Diego. However, by the time they arrived, much of the fighting had ended. Several remained and created Mormon settlements near San Bernadino, California. Others headed north and were among the early participants in the gold rush near Sacramento.

The Mormon Mail

Mormons were among the first to carry the U.S. mail across America. Before the coming of the railroad, the mail was carried by pioneer wagon trains or by ship to California. In 1850, the first U.S. mail service began between Salt Lake City and places east. In 1851, a Mormon named Feramorz Little took the U.S. mail contract. His task was to ride 500 miles across the plains to Laramie, Wyoming, every month on the 15th and exchange the packs of mail going west and east. Often he had to ride further, to Independence, Missouri, or even Washington, D.C.

Little hired two other Mormon men, Eph Hanks and Charley Decker, to help him make the grueling 2,400-mile ride each month to Independence and back again to Salt Lake City, a journey of 40 to 50 days. From 1851 to 1857, these rugged men made about 100 trips across the plains on horseback. They rode in dust, heat, hail, and snow, with little food other than rabbit, badger, squirrel, or buffalo meat along the way. These early mailmen encountered dangerous adventures with bears, wild animals, swift rivers, and hostile Native Americans. They learned native languages and customs, making friends with several tribes, giving aid, performing healings, and fostering understanding; other times they had to ride for their lives.

These mailmen often escorted important travelers, government officials, even relatives of U.S. presidents. Brigham Young wanted the Mormons to carry the mail coast to coast, so Hanks also made mail trips to California; when the snow was taller than the horses, he walked on snowshoes. One time, as Little wrote in his 1884 book *Mail Service Across the Plains*, Decker "had to swim every river between this and Laramie . . . in the ice water with the mail all the time." Another time, Hanks and his raft were "sucked under, forcing them to swim for their lives; the mail was carried down the stream and lay in the water upward to two hours. At the risk of their lives, they secured it." These Mormon mailmen helped establish a regular mail service across America, aiding communication, culture, and travel.

In 1857, the Mormon mail service, now known as the "Brigham Young Express," wanted to carry freight from Salt Lake City to Independence, but the federal government canceled the contract due to tensions between Congress and the Mormons, events that led to the Utah War (see page 40). By 1860, the Wells Fargo Company stagecoach became the preferred way to travel across the plains and carry the U.S.

DISASTER ON THE TRAIL

Thousands of Latter-day Saints crossed the plains using wagons, horses, or walking with small, lightweight handcarts. Eight companies of people using these handcarts successfully crossed the plains, but two ended in tragedy. In 1856, the Martin and Willie cart companies became the largest disaster of any of the emigrant groups, with 222 people dying of hunger, fatigue, and exposure.

Early mailman
The Mormon mail delivery service preceded the establishment of the Pony Express, here shown in a modern recreation.

mail. The Pony Express was also active at this time; many Mormon men and boys rode for the service. The 1861 arrival of the telegraph and the 1869 completion of the transcontinental railroad brought horse-carried mail to an end, but not the memory of the riders' early role in linking the country.

Mormons and the Arts

Young wanted Mormons to develop their own arts and culture, so he sent gifted Church members back East or to Europe to study everything from medicine to painting to architecture. He sent artists and architects to Europe on "art missions" to learn from masters. In the 1850s, Young sent architect Truman O. Angell (1810–1887) to Europe to study Gothic cathedrals and houses of parliament to help him design the Salt Lake Temple. Angell was inspired by St. Peter's Basilica at the Vatican in Rome. In 1890, a few Mormon artists went to Paris on an art mission to prepare for painting the murals inside the Salt Lake Temple. John

Mormon Innovators

Along with helping develop the transcontinental mail service, Mormons were involved in a wide variety of other innovations. Here are a few examples:

• Mormon pioneers invented a device to count the miles as they crossed the prairie in the 1847 western migration (see page 37). Using two round wooden cogs attached to their wagon's wheels, fellow pioneers William Clayton and Orson Pratt were able to count the wheels' revolutions and thus the distance traveled. Clayton counted the distance and marked the trail with signposts every 10 miles—making early road signs across the American plains. He also published an Emigrants' Guide, which listed major landmarks along the Mormon Trail and the miles between each one. Their innovative device lives on in spirit today as an odometer, found in most road vehicles to measure distance traveled.

• The first electric traffic signal in the world was invented by a Salt Lake City policeman, Lester Wire, in 1918. It was installed at the intersection of Main Street and 200 South in downtown Salt Lake City and resembled a "wire birdhouse," so the locals called it "Wire's pigeon house."

• After Richmond, Virginia, Salt Lake City was the second U.S. city to have electric trolley cars, in 1889. Launched by Walter Reed, a Mormon who crossed the plains as a little boy, the Salt Lake trolley system was heralded in 1908 as the model street-car system for the rest of the country, and other cities patterned their trolley systems after it. The historic trolley car barns and water tower still stand on Trolley Square, six blocks south of Temple Square in Salt Lake City.

• Philo Farnsworth (1906–1971), a Mormon, was 20 years old when he invented the television. He also invented the electronic microscope, as well as pioneering black light and radar. In 1926, shortly after leaving Brigham Young University to work in California, Farnsworth produced the first all-electronic television image.

Hafen, J. B. Fairbanks, Lorus Pratt, Edwin Evans, and Dan Weggeland painted the huge murals on the temple walls in the French impressionist style.

Mormon artists bring a sense of faith to their art, and an optimism in the face of suffering. Historically, Mormon art is not an expression of doubt or pain, but a witness or testimony. The Brigham Young statue on Temple Square facing Main Street in Salt Lake City reaches out to all passing by; it was sculpted by LDS artist Cyrus Dallin (1861–1944) and placed in 1897. The angel Moroni statue seen atop most LDS temples was sculpted by Avard Fairbanks (1897–1989), a Mormon who painted portraits of notable individuals from around the world. C.C.A. Christensen made paintings of Mormon and Utah life, that often appeared in the magazine *Art in America*. Minerva Teichert painted Mormon themes and Book of Mormon scenes. Arnold Friberg illustrated the Book of Mormon, giving life to the Nephites and Lamanites. Mahonri Young sculpted the "This is the place" monument (named for Young's famous statement as he overlooked the Salt Lake Valley) in 1947 as a tribute to Mormon pioneers; it is located at the mouth of Emigration Canyon and, has been visited by millions. Convert Gary Smith sculpted statues of men, women, and children seen in Nauvoo and Utah, depicting scenes of Mormon family life. And the paintings of LDS artist Trevor Southey humanize angelic visitations to Joseph Smith, while rendering human forms more ethereal.

Brigham Young University has sponsored an Annual Mormon Arts Festival since 1969, to encourage LDS playwrights, painters, sculptors, and composers.

Mormon Symbols in Art

Mormonism uses no icons or images of holy figures or people on in its chapels. These figures appear only on its early temples and historic buildings. Icons (images of holy people or objects) were used in early Mormonism, such as all-seeing-eyes, clasped hands, suns, moons, stars, clouds, keys, and wheat, but are no longer used today. The one symbol or icon used by modern Mormonism is the angel Moroni (see page 26).

Unlike other Christian faiths, the LDS Church does not use the cross, which Mormons see as a symbol of suffering or the means by which Jesus died, and thus not an uplifting image. Also, the cross is a symbol of traditional Christianity, which Mormonism does not identify with, since Mormons believe the LDS Church is "restored" Christianity.

Instead, both art and holy places use images of the angel Moroni, whom Smith saw in a vision bringing the "restored Gospel" and the gold plates from which he translated the Book of Mormon. Today, a gold-plated angel Moroni is the symbol placed atop LDS temples. Mormons identify Moroni as the "angel of the restoration" mentioned in the New Testament book of Revelation (14:6): "I saw another angel fly, having the everlasting gospel to preach to the inhabitants of the earth."

Another symbol of Mormonism and Utah is the beehive, which represents work, industry, and community. Bees are always busy working together for the good of the hive, each having a role in the community and supporting the queen, together producing results that are nourishing to all. The angel and beehive represent the two aspects of

A temple of art
The beautiful Salt Lake Temple features a gold statue of the angel Moroni blowing a trumpet atop the highest of its six spires.

Mormonism—spiritual and material, divine and physical. The beehive appears as a symbol on many buildings in Utah, while the angel Moroni appears on Mormon temples and is used as a symbol on Church publications, materials, and objects.

Mormon Theater

Dramatic performance is a core aspect of Mormon culture: Prophetic orations, elaborate pageants, local plays, and public speaking to large audiences remind viewers that the church is often a stage. Joseph Smith and Brigham Young both valued theater as a part of community life and plays were performed at the Nauvoo Masonic Hall, where Young played the lead in one play.

In 1862, Young established the Salt Lake Theater, where Utah's noted actress, Maude Adams (1872–1953), performed. Young's nephew Morris Young performed in drag (women's clothing) in a play called

Madame Paderini. Mormon drama continued with the Promised Valley Playhouse and its musical *Promised Valley*, by Arnold Sundgaard and Crawford Gates, which was performed regularly from 1947 to 1996. Other popular plays that feature Mormon themes or events from LDS Church history include *Saturday's Warriors* (1973) by Doug Stewart and Lex de Azevedo, *Here's Brother Brigham* (1976) by James Arrington, and *Huebner* (1980) by Thomas Rogers.

Since 1970, some Mormon actors and themes have begun to reach national audiences. Large theatrical pageants are performed in Rochester, New York; Palmyra, Utah; and Oakland, California, depicting Joseph Smith receiving the golden plates that became the Book of Mormon. The Salt Lake Acting Co. showcases LDS writers and themes, including an annual satire of Mormon culture called *Saturday's Voyeur*. A one-woman stage show by Carol Lynn Pearson, *Mother Wove the Morning* (1989), toured across the United States for several years.

Mormon themes have even made it to Broadway. The 1994 Tony Award-winning play *Angels in America* by Tony Kushner used Mormonism's angel motif and Mormon characters to explore social tensions in American culture.

A Variety of Mormon Products

Mormonism developed a material culture early, with sacred objects like seer stones (special rocks said to have the power to predict the future), parchments, scriptures, holy oil, and sacred clothing.

All Mormon towns in the West—beginning with Salt Lake City and spreading outward—have a unique Latter-day Saints character. You will find neat brick buildings, stone halls, and temples. Every Mormon village was laid out on Smith's "plat of Zion" with a square grid of streets, numbered from a center square where a church or temple was built (*plat* is a term for a map or chart of a piece of land). Each town's buildings embodied the religion, with a bishop's storehouse, a Relief Society hall and granary, a co-op store, a social hall, and a school. Utah's historic towns still show their pioneer heritage with streets on a grid and 19th-century Mormon brick buildings. Nauvoo, Illinois, and Utah's Sanpete County are two of the few intact Mormon historical districts.

Along with planning the cities, early Mormons filled them with various goods. Frontier homesteading arts and handicrafts included homemade quilts, clothes, rag rugs, and home-grown woven silk. A Mormon handicraft store was established in 1938 to sell "women's work" (homemade crafts) to outsiders, and still operates today in Salt Lake City. Homemade Mormon quilts are collector's items.

Later, Mormon culture expanded and merged with the wider 1950s American culture. Mormons became known for their beehive hairdos, gelatin molds, Kerr canning jars filled with fruit, framed pictures of LDS temples and prophets, vinyl scripture tote bags, and rings with the initials CTR ("choose the right"). Other popular Mormon products include Franklin Quest day planners (business diaries) and Covey employee and management training seminars that help businesses improve their efficiency (company founder Stephen Covey is a prominent and successful LDS member; see page 108).

Mormons have pioneered new foods, such as French fry sauce, honey butter and hot scones, root beer, and Jell-O salads. Utah leads the nation in ice cream and Jell-O consumption; the Mormon corridor of towns from Idaho to Arizona captures Mormon culture so well, it is nicknamed "the Jell-O belt." A&W brand root beer was created by

Keeping organized
The Utah-based Franklin Covey company, founded and led by Mormons, produces datebooks, business diaries, and personal organizers such as this one.

a Mormon man who became a millionaire; today, J. Willard Marriott (see page 104) owns hotel chains, restaurants, and food services that can be found all around the globe.

Impact on Literature

Mormonism's first and major contribution to American literature was the Book of Mormon (published in 1830). The Book of Mormon appeared during the birth of a national American literature, reaching thousands of readers across the nation, and sharing American themes with other early books. Within a decade, the book was being read in England. In 1844, copies reached the South Pacific islands. By 1850, thousands of people in Britain, Scandinavia, and Europe were reading the book. To date, the LDS Church says more than 100 million copies of the Book of Mormon have been published.

The Mormon impact on more recent literature is more varied, as these stories of three successful authors demonstrate.

Richard Paul Evans is a Mormon author who used his own marketing skills to create a best-selling story. After submitting his book *The Christmas Box* to several publishers and being turned down by all of them, Evans decided to self-publish his book. It was an enormous success. The book tells the story of a widow and the young family that moves in with her; together they have a moving experience of the message of Christmas.

Evans' sentimental story had great popular appeal, and his unique marketing strategies surprised the publishing world. He first published the book in a small pocket-sized edition, perfect for stuffing in Christmas stockings, and also placed copies in small but attention-grabbing green cardboard displays on bookstore counters near the cash registers. Since then, that book and several sequels have been published with great success by Simon & Schuster. A television movie version was in the works in 2002, and Evans has used some of the profits of his work to establish his own publishing company, as well as the Christmas Box House children's charity.

Orson Scott Card (b.1951) is one of the most successful science fiction writers in the United States today. A graduate of Brigham Young University and a former LDS missionary in Brazil, Card was the first LDS writer to win the Hugo and Nebula awards for best science fiction novel, which he won in 2000 and 2001. Among his bestsellers are *Ender's*

Game (1986), *Speaker for the Dead* (1987), and *Ender's Shadow* (1999). Card's series of books featuring the Alvin Maker character are loosely based on Joseph Smith and Mormon themes.

Terry Tempest Williams (b.1955) is the author of the bestseller *Refuge* and several other books. She specializes in a new style of memoir. She focuses on the material, physical world around her, hoping to save it from destruction, ignorance, and insensitivity, by increasing her own sensitivity to all things. Williams is one of the best-known female Mormon authors in America today. She discusses Mormon themes in some of her work and imbeds her Mormon values and heritage in her narratives.

The bestselling British mystery writer Anne Perry, author of a series of books that feature detectives who work in Victorian England, is also a Mormon.

Education and Mormon Life

Knowledge is salvation in the Mormon faith, and education is part of that process. Smith wrote in The Doctrine and Covenants, "A man is saved no faster than he gains knowledge," and "The glory of God is intelligence." He envisioned a University of Nauvoo to "enable us to teach our children wisdom, to instruct them in all the knowledge and learning."

This vision did not materialize in his lifetime, but did take shape later in Utah as the University of Deseret (now called the University of Utah), founded by Brigham Young in 1850. The University of Utah helped develop the first artificial heart, and its Primary Children's Hospital, created by the LDS Church in 1922, is a leading pediatrics center in the United States.

The Mormons had to create their own schools for children in the Great Basin they settled, and also high schools for their youth. Brigham Young Academy (1875) became the first of 33 LDS academies from Canada to Mexico. Today Brigham Young University (BYU), as it is now known, is the largest private university in the United States. The BYU main campus in Provo, Utah, has 30,000 students, and sponsors additional campuses in Hawaii, Idaho, and Jerusalem.

The Church Educational System (CES), found in 144 countries and territories, provides religious instruction for more than 375,000 high school students and 265,000 college-age students. In underprivi-

MORMONS IN SPORTS
Here are some prominent Mormons from the world of professional sports.

Danny Ainge, baseball, basketball

Thurl Bailey, basketball

Billy Casper, golf

Ty Detmer, football

Johnny Miller, golf

Larry H. Miller, basketball team owner

Dale Murphy, baseball

Merlin Olsen, football

Peter Vidmar, gymnastics

Steve Young, football

leged areas where public schools are not available, the LDS Church has been offering schooling since 1977. It now operates 10,000 elementary or secondary schools in Mexico, South America, and Polynesia.

In Utah, the focus on education gave rise to other colleges and universities around the state. Various studies have concluded that Utah produces more scientists and scholars per capita than any other state, and that many have made significant contributions in their fields, especially in agriculture and science.

The Mormon Tabernacle Choir

One of the best-known cultural endeavors of the LDS Church is the world-famous Mormon Tabernacle Choir. The Tabernacle Choir is known for its size and heavenly sound, created by 360 voices all harmonizing perfectly. The choir takes its name from the large, domed Tabernacle on Temple Square—built in 1867 and known for its perfect acoustics. Inside the Tabernacle you can hear a pin drop and gaze upon the famous Tabernacle Organ with its 11,623 pipes, all painted gold.

The choir was formed shortly after the Mormons first arrived in the Salt Lake Valley in 1847, when a small church choir sang on land that is now Temple Square. The Tabernacle Choir is best known for its Sunday morning radio broadcast *Music and the Spoken Word*, aired from the Tabernacle every Sunday morning at 9:30 A.M. This program has been an American tradition since 1929, and is now carried on 2,000 radio, television, and cable stations across the United States.

The choir has made more than 150 recordings, including gold and platinum albums and a Grammy award-winning version of "The

Battle Hymn of the Republic." The choir tours the world and has performed in concert halls of Europe, Mexico, South America, Canada, Japan, Australia, Israel, and Russia. The choir has also performed for several U.S. presidents at inaugural ceremonies and in the White House.

The Mormon Image in American Culture

The Mormon image has changed dramatically over two centuries from negative to positive. Originally seen as struggling in New York's frontier villages, as opportunists in Ohio, then as dangerous extremists in Missouri, and ambitious idealists in 1840s Nauvoo—the early views of Mormons were often negative. This gave birth to anti-Mormon literature, such as E.D. Howe's *Mormonism Unveiled* (1836).

Things got worse when the Mormons went West. In the 1850s through 1890s the LDS pioneers were seen as primitive polygamists with harems of wives. The Mormons were considered bizarre and extreme by many non-Mormons, and anti-Mormon images in newspapers, magazines, and cartoons depicted polygamy. At the same time, some found Utah compelling, such as British explorer Sir Richard Burton (1821–1890), who wrote *City of the Saints* (1861), or President Abraham Lincoln, who predicted that Utah would become a treasure trove of the Union.

Only after polygamy was abandoned in 1890 (see page 46) did the Mormon image begin to shift from negative to positive. A key change in the image of Mormons then came in 1929 when the Mormon Tabernacle Choir began broadcasting the radio program *Music and the Spoken Word.*

The Mormon image became quite positive after World War II, and especially in the 1950s, when Mormon culture became more in tune with American culture. In the 1960s and 1970s, Mormon advertisements in *Reader's Digest* and commercials on television have conveyed a warm, positive image of a traditional home and nuclear family. Today, while they remain in some ways insular, the Mormons are paying continuing attention to creating a positive image for their faith and their people.

From Peculiar to Interesting

The Mormon religion seems to be coming of age in American culture, no longer regarded as bizarre or peculiar, but as a fascinating and

MORMONS IN THE ARTS

Here is a list of Mormons who are or were prominent in various areas of the arts:

FILM

Don Bluth, animator

Richard Dutcher, director

Dean Jagger, actor

Neil LaBute, director

Natasha Rambova, actress

Sam Taylor, screenwriter

TELEVISION

Billy Barty, actor

Eliza Dushku, actress

Philo T. Farnsworth, inventor of television

Lorne Greene, actor

Gordon Jump, actor

Donny and Marie Osmond, entertainers

MUSIC

Randy Bachman, The Guess Who and Bachman-Turner Overdrive

The King Family, singers

Gladys Knight, singer

The Mormon Tabernacle Choir

The Osmond Brothers

Brother and sister act
The widespread popular appeal of Donny and Marie Osmond and the other members of the Osmond Family of entertainers helped improve the image of Mormons in America.

significant American subculture. This probably began in the 1950s when the LDS Church jelled as a culture, then took root in the 1970s and 1980s, in large part thanks to the Osmond family of singers and entertainers (see page 108).

In the 1990s, Mormonism seems to have arrived in American culture, as Mormon characters and themes are found in movies, television, books, and plays. From the *Bob Newhart Show* in the 1970s with its character Norman Borden ("the Mormon Doorman"), to references on *The Simpsons*, to television shows about polygamy or an *X-Files* episode based on Mormon history, to a number of movies about Mormons in 2001, the faith is finding its place in American discourse.

In 1957, writer Thomas O'Dea said in his book *The Mormons*, "Mormondom became a subculture with its own peculiar conceptions and values, its own self- consciousness, and its own culture area." And what is that culture? It is a Mormon world view—a view of life and the world seen through Mormon lenses shaped by LDS theology, doctrine, and history.

4

The Mormon Church in American Society

TODAY, THE LDS CHURCH STANDS FOR HIGH PERSONAL STANDARDS, conservative family values, prosperity, and clean living. The Mormons combined an industrious work ethic with Joseph Smith's vision and Brigham Young's organizational skills to build from scratch a society that soon attracted many new members. The Latter-day Saints banded together to become political and economic leaders in their part of the West, with their communities reaching from Mexico to Canada before the end of the 19th century.

However, throughout much of their 170-year history, the Mormons have found themselves at odds with their non-Mormon neighbors, as they seek recognition for their impressive accomplishments and a stamp of legitimacy for their religion. The Church has come a long way from the first generation of Mormons, who fled from settlement to settlement to build Zion, or God's kingdom on earth.

American religious life was in great transition in 1830. Independent preachers roamed the countrysides; one common theme among them was the ever-nearing end of the world. Smith's message that people basically were good and that all can achieve divine status in the next life appealed to a variety of religious seekers. However, Smith's revelations about Jesus were radically different from mainstream Christianity. While his devoted followers trusted him, non-Mormons became nervous, then, as we saw in chapter 2, violently angry when Smith's ideas spread through the areas where Mormons gathered.

America hosted a variety of religious viewpoints, and the Mormons might have been left alone if not for the community plans Smith put into action. In their Ohio, Missouri, and then Illinois settlements, Latter-day Saints formed their own economic network, relying exclusively on one another's businesses. Their earnings went to the Church, which dispersed it as needed. That enabled the Mormons to prosper as a group and help newly arriving converts. But it angered other local businesspeople, whose shops were ignored by the Mormons.

Zealous Mormon converts were openly and sometimes aggressively certain that their faith was the religion on the righteous path to salvation. Also, relations between European-American settlers and Native Americans often were tense. Friendship between Native Americans and Mormons made non-Mormons uneasy.

The Most Radical Revelation

Before they crossed the plains and mountains to get to Utah, the Mormons built a remarkable city, Nauvoo, on a swamp along the Mississippi River in Illinois. Within two years, by 1841, the Mormons had drained the swampland and erected hundreds of buildings made from lumber hauled from Church-owned timber camps in Wisconsin.

Anxious for Mormon votes, the Illinois state legislature granted Smith a city charter allowing the Mormons to form their own court system and militia, with Smith in charge. Plans were made to build a grand temple. Again, distrustful neighbors grew uneasy. Smith appeared to be building an exclusive empire which only continued to get larger. And when he began discussing revelations from God about polygamy, he repelled Mormon outsiders as well as many Mormons, who left to form another church based on the Book of Mormon.

It was thought that Smith's murder in 1844 (see page 32) would be the end of the Latter-day Saints. But his close associate, Brigham Young, was determined to make sure the Church, with its thousands of members, survived. Under Young's tightly controlled leadership, and finally far away from potential enemies, the Church of Jesus Christ of Latter-day Saints thrived in Utah. It would also continue to rub Americans the wrong way for decades to come.

PRECEDING PAGE
Family man
This 1875 photograph shows an unidentified Mormon man with his two wives and nine children. The issue of polygamy played a big part in the early history of the Church of Jesus Christ of Latter-day Saints.

A Scandal Emerges

Mormon pioneers surged into Utah by wagon train and on foot. Their exceptional organizational skills and devotion to the tasks ahead of them quickly made Salt Lake City a desert oasis with sturdy homes, schools, and churches. The United States government made Utah an official territory in 1850, with Young installed as governor.

In 1852, however, Young publicly announced what non-Mormons had suspected for years: the Church practiced polygamy. From the beginning, Smith had directed Church members to obey the "laws of the land." There was no federal law against polygamy. That would soon change, however, and Mormons would find their achievements in Utah always overshadowed by what they called "the Principle."

Considering polygamy a divine directive because it was revealed to Smith by God, Mormons promoted it as a positive family structure. Smith married 27 women and Young did the same (he fathered 56 children). The official record for the most number of wives was 43. Outsiders assumed all Mormon men practiced polygamy, but actually only 10 to 20 percent of Mormon men did. Practicing "the Principle" was mandatory for prominent Mormon church leaders or businessmen, and most of them added just one additional wife.

Young's 1852 announcement became national news. He expected polygamy to be tolerated, perhaps even imitated, and was taken aback by the strong reaction against it. For many outsiders it was a curiosity. Tourists began arriving in Salt Lake City hoping to catch a glimpse of multiple wives coming and going from Lion House, Young's large home.

But news of polygamy was also taken seriously. When the Republican Party was formed in 1854, it vowed to fight slavery and polygamy, what it called "the twin relics of barbarism." The federal government removed Young as Utah's governor in 1857, and in 1862 Congress passed a law prohibiting polygamy in the United States, including its territories.

For awhile the law was not enforced—the Civil War kept the federal government busy, and Utah juries usually consisted of Mormons. Plural marriages were performed secretly, with no public records. Anti-Mormons found another way to strike by making it illegal to "cohabitate," or live with members of the opposite sex outside of marriage.

The issue of polygamy was not going to go away. Mormon leaders staunchly defended it, and non-Mormons considered it unacceptable.

POLYGAMISTS TODAY

Although the LDS Church formally ended polygamy in 1890, an estimated 30,000 people, some claiming to be "fundamentalist" Mormons, live in polygamous families in and around Utah today. One recent case receiving wide publicity involved Tom Green, who dared prosecutors to go after him by appearing on national television and radio programs. "The only thing I'm guilty of is building my family according to my religious beliefs," said Green, the father of 30 children, on National Public Radio's (NPR) *Talk of the Nation* in July 2000.

Utah officials often ignored polygamous families. After all, pointed out NPR reporter Howard Berkes in that report, "Many people in this state have polygamy in their ancestry, and many prosecutors do as well." It seemed a crime without a victim—adults choosing a way of life. But when stories emerged of young girls forced into polygamous marriages, prosecutors began cracking down.

Green was convicted in 2001 of four counts of bigamy (marriage to more than one person) and was ordered to repay welfare payments of more than $78,000.

Leaving the country or marrying secretly became the only way Mormon men could practice polygamy. Young died in 1877, leaving behind a growing, stable Church community that would not have to move again. He also left the issue of polygamy unresolved, and it has continued to plague the Church to the present day.

Latter-day Saints wanted to be considered respectable Americans and recognized for their significant contribution to the development of the western United States. They also wanted to practice their religion just as they saw fit. They could not have both, and by 1890 church leaders began reconsidering polygamy. In a Church announcement in 1890, Mormon president Wilford Woodruff asked Mormons to refrain from entering into new plural marriages and encouraged more interaction with non-Mormons (see page 88 for more details on the Manifesto). U.S. president Benjamin Harrison granted amnesty to all currently polygamous Mormons and Utah celebrated when, on January 4, 1896, it was granted statehood.

But the issue of polygamy never really went away. Mormons who continued to enter into plural marriages after the Church denounced it were—and are—excommunicated (exiled from the Church and its practices), but the issue remains. Although there are now millions of law-abiding Mormons in the world, the association of polygamy with the Latter-day Saints is a stamp that still has not faded.

Role of Women in the Church

The position of women in the Mormon Church was most prominent in its early days and was unique among American women in Utah's pioneer era. As Mormons became more comfortable in the 20th century, the role of women in Mormon communities came to resemble that of other American women, whose lives revolved around marriage and family. Of course there are exceptions, but this characterization generally still holds true today, as the Church of Jesus Christ of Latter-day Saints presents itself as a champion of traditional values.

The first female Mormon, Smith's wife Emma Hale Smith (1804–1879), ardently supported her husband. Emma was Joseph's first scribe as he orally translated the golden plates from behind a blanket hanging between them. In Nauvoo, Joseph encouraged Emma to organize the all-female Relief Society. She and other wives pooled often-meager resources to assist Mormons in need. But Emma did not accompa-

Women at work
The Relief Society has long been the main way that women contribute to LDS Church activities. This 1890 photo shows society members at work sorting flowers.

ny the Mormons on the trek to Utah. Adamantly opposed to polygamy, she and the Smiths' children stayed behind in Illinois. Their descendants remain prominent in the Reorganized LDS Church, a separate Mormon church based in Missouri.

Fighting for Women's Right to Vote

In Nauvoo and in early Utah days Mormon missionaries were almost exclusively married men. While the men traveled their territories, their wives were expected to raise their children and keep a farm or business going, perhaps for several years and under often-difficult conditions.

The Utah Territory was distinctive in granting women voting rights in 1870. This added Mormon votes to the ballots to keep Church members in political offices.

It was not unusual for Mormon women to have careers in that era, too, especially "plural" wives (wives of polygamous husbands). Emmaline Blanche Woodward was the seventh wife of Mormon leader Daniel Wells. She became the editor of a Mormon newspaper, the

Woman's Exponent, which became a passionate voice for women's rights and suffrage (the right to vote). She spent several months lobbying for that right in Washington, D.C., before Utah's law giving women the vote was repealed by the national government in 1887.

The Relief Society is almost as old as the Church, and has always been a place for Mormon women who relish opportunities to lead, although its agenda requires approval of the male heads of the Church. Today the organization has nearly 5 million members worldwide, making it one of the largest women's organizations anywhere.

All Mormons are encouraged to marry and raise children, because the Church continues to assert that a woman's most valued job is as a mother. "Marriage is essential to His [God's] eternal plan," and when it comes to parenting, "mothers are primarily responsible for the nurture of their children," said an official proclamation read by Church president Gordon B. Hinckley in 1995.

Women who challenge the traditional viewpoint of the Church can find themselves excommunicated from the Church or fired from teaching jobs at Mormon-run universities. However, revision of the endowment temple ceremony (see page 21) is one concession the Church has made to female Mormons in recent years. Mormons believe the endowment ritual will bond them with God for eternity. The Church eliminated from the ceremony a required promise by the wife to obey her husband, and women also are no longer required to cover their heads with veils during the ceremony.

Many Mormon women are content with the contributions they can offer their Church under its current structure. "We can alter the face of the earth one family at a time, and one home at a time," said Relief Society officer Anne Pingree at a society convention in 2002.

Minorities in the Church

American minorities have played a role in the Mormon Church from its beginning. Native Americans were considered "brethren," or brothers. The Book of Mormon describes them as descended from lost tribes of Israel. The Mormons befriended local Native Americans when possible, and had fewer conflicts with them in the West than most other white pioneers. Native Mexicans living outside of Catholic-influenced larger cities became eager converts to Mormonism, and today Mexico has nearly 900,000 LDS Church members.

In recent decades Church officials reversed the long-standing rule against African-American men attaining the position of priesthood. The first Mormons were from northern states and welcomed African Americans into the Church. Although it did not make up a significant number, black membership became an issue when the Mormons arrived in Missouri, a state where slavery was legal. Missourians balked at the thought of an increasing number of free African Americans there. Smith, abiding by the law of the land, spoke out against abolition of slavery in Missouri, but reversed his position in Nauvoo, where he advocated its peaceful end.

It was Young, once in Utah, who firmly denied the right of African-American men to earn LDS priesthood. Young claimed as the reason a theory, popular among many white southern religious leaders, that Africans were descended from Ham, son of the Biblical figure Noah and cursed by God. Ham's descendants, it was taught, were doomed to perpetual servant status.

Nevertheless, a small number of blacks remained in the Church, some accompanying the first wagon trains West. Nor did the rule stop missionaries from working to convert black people in South America and Africa in the 20th century. In 1978 Church Apostle LeGrand Richards noted that black Brazilian Church members were raising money for a new temple they would not be allowed to enter because of LDS policy. That summer, Church president Spencer Kimball announced through the Church office that he had received a revelation that "every faithful, worthy man in the Church may receive the holy priesthood."

Today, the Mormon Church claims members on almost every continent. It has been especially successful in Latin America, which accounts for almost half of the total worldwide LDS Church membership.

Today's Mormon Missionaries

By the 1930s, Mormon communities were organizing outside the Salt Lake Basin, as wards formed in the south and in California. And missionaries took the Mormon message throughout America and beyond. Here is the story of a more recent missionary.

Gavin Pouliot, 19, is one of three children of Mike and Shauna Pouliot in Portsmouth, New Hampshire. Like most Mormon missionaries, Gavin is a male high school graduate postponing college to work as a missionary away from home. He held down two jobs to earn enough

Missionary work
Young members of the LDS Church, mostly men, go on missions when they are about 19 years old. Many are sent to foreign countries, such as Mexico, above. The young men travel in pairs and are usually seen wearing ties and neat white shirts.

money to support himself for two years in England. His father was not a missionary in his youth, but now serves as the president of a New England stake, or Church district. Mike and Shauna plan to become missionaries themselves when their children are older. The Pouliot family was profiled on January 23, 2002, by their local newspaper, the *Portsmouth Herald*, as "ideal members" of the Mormon Church.

Missionaries have been a big part of the Mormon Church from its earliest days. Smith moved his flock from New York to Kirtland, Ohio, when Mormon missionaries converted an entire church congregation there in 1831. Later, missionaries leaving Nauvoo and Utah had great success in England and Scandinavia. Converts from those countries emigrated to America and streamed into Salt Lake City, aided by a special fund established by Young to build up Zion.

Today, Gavin Pouliot represents an estimated 60,000 volunteer Mormon missionaries working in more than 200 countries around the world. Three-fourths of them are young men between the ages of 19 and 26. They always travel in pairs, usually wearing neat white shirts and dark pants.

They serve for about two years, and as elders of the Church they can baptize new members. About 18 percent of missionary Mormons are young women, and about 7 percent are married couples.

While in England, Pouliot and his male missionary partner will not be allowed to date. Missionaries are discouraged from watching television or listening to the radio in their host country, and are asked not to call home more than two or three times a year. In the future, as a former missionary, Pouliot will be eligible for discounted tuition at Brigham Young University.

Mormons and Genealogy

You could say that Latter-day Saints take their mission work out of this world—literally. If a Church member's ancestors were not Mormons in their earthly lives, it does not mean they cannot become Mormons now. In other words, the Church teaches that people who died without learning of or accepting the Mormon faith have the opportunity to do so in the spirit world. Living Mormons stand in for deceased family members and undergo baptism, confirmation, and eternal marriage ceremonies for them. In order to baptize as many of their ancestors as possible, the Mormons have accumulated extensive genealogical (family history) records that non-Mormons have access to, as well.

The Latter-day Saints formed a genealogical research society in 1894 and in the 1940s began using microfilm to record birth, marriage, and death records from around the United States and the world. These records are kept in huge storage vaults deep in granite mountains near Salt Lake City—vaults designed to withstand a nuclear blast.

Interest in genealogy has soared among all Americans in recent years, and the general public has made much use of the Mormon's Family History Library in Salt Lake City. Family researchers can browse through millions of volumes of vital statistics there or at hundreds of other Family History Centers around the world (local stakes or wards can be contacted for locations). The Internet has also become an important genealogical tool for the LDS Church and for private citizens researching their roots.

Mobilizing Members on Traditional Views of Marriage

The Mormon Church has also tried to galvanize members about what it considers to be another threat to traditional family values: gay rights.

ANOTHER KIND OF MISSIONARY

Young men, women, and married couples serve as Mormon missionaries. But football players?

Students—and, it follows, student athletes—at BYU are assumed to be Latter-day Saints. The more success BYU athletes attain, the more exposure for them and the Church. BYU athletic director Val Hale told the *Salt Lake Tribune* on September 29, 2002, that his athletes "try to be a good example so that people around the country will . . . hopefully have interest in the Church."

To further the goal of publicity via sports, the university is funneling $50 million into its athletic program. With all that money on the line, school officials want BYU teams to rank nationally in the top 20.

In 1998 California's 750,000 resident Mormons received letters from Church leaders asking for money to help support passage of a state ballot initiative, the Definition of Marriage Act, that would exclude homosexuals from the legal definition of marriage—a cause the Church also took up in Hawaii and Alaska.

The Utah state legislature, 90 percent of whose members are Mormon, spent several weeks in the winter of 1996 working to find a way to keep a recently formed gay and lesbian student group from meeting at a Salt Lake City high school. Ironically, it was Utah senator Orrin Hatch (see page 106) who made it easier for the new club to form. In 1984 he successfully sponsored the federal Equal Access Act, requiring public schools to allow meetings for all clubs. Hatch wanted to make sure Bible clubs were not excluded from extracurricular schedules. Now, the Equal Access Act made it possible for homosexual high school students to form a club, too, much to the chagrin of the Utah legislature. In the end, they passed a law banning any club "devoted to bigotry, criminal activity" or pertaining to "human sexuality."

In Utah Mormons still have the most success at legislating their religious beliefs. As of 2002, Utah's governor was Mormon, as were all of the state's Supreme Court justices and 80 percent of Utah's state and federal judges. Mayors, country commissioners, school superintendents, and board members throughout the state tend to be Mormon.

The Mormon work ethic has created a highly productive work force, and the Church's tradition of making schools a priority in new settlement has left Utah's youth among the best educated in America. In the 1930s Church president Heber Grant (1856–1945) reintroduced the 100-year-old "word of wisdom," Smith's advice to avoid alcohol, tobacco, and caffeine. Today there are no bars and nightclubs in Salt Lake City (although there are private clubs that serve alcohol) and its suburbs, which helps give Utah communities an enviably low crime rate.

Balancing American Freedoms and Mormon Values

Mormon society is family friendly indeed, but to the increasing number of non-Mormons moving to Utah, conforming to Church ways can be difficult. "I have to wonder if I am a citizen of Salt Lake City or the Mormon Church! Should I pay taxes or tithing?" wondered one Utah resident in a letter to the *Salt Lake Tribune* in October 2002. Young advised "those that don't like our looks and our customs" to go elsewhere. But those customs are more difficult to enforce these days.

One recent example: The Mormon Church purchased an outdoor plaza area from the city, but the sale required the Church to allow it to remain a public thoroughfare. The Church attempted to restrict behavior and dress (no smoking, protesting, or objectionable clothing) of those walking through the plaza, but a federal circuit court ruled that the church could only impose restrictions on the plaza if the city gave up its public sidewalk through the area—which violated the Church's purchase agreement with the city.

Critics charge that LDS Church restrictions on the plaza are a heavy-handed violation of free speech. Supporters say that the rules are an attempt to establish beneficial boundaries between acceptable and unacceptable behaviors. A person does not have to be Mormon, for instance, to appreciate sitting outdoors in a public space that is free of cigarette smoke and loud music. The debate over the plaza points out the kind of issues that Utah, with its strong Mormon presence, probably wrestles with more than other American states.

The 2002 Winter Olympics

Just as the Mormons spent decades lobbying for Utah's statehood, a century later they were thrilled when Salt Lake City was named as the site for the 2002 Winter Olympics. City officials began vying for the honor in 1966. Because of the close association between the Mormon Church and Salt Lake City, some commentators wondered if the event would become a showcase for Mormons to spread their faith. But LDS president Gordon Hinckley vowed the Church would not use the event to preach to non-Mormons. Rather, Church leaders considered having all eyes on Salt Lake City for two or three weeks to be an opportunity to showcase positive aspects of Mormon life in Utah.

The Olympics proved to be a mixed blessing. As the Games approached, a controversy arose over how the decision was made by the International Olympic Committee (IOC). Some of the organizers were accused—and in fact indicted—for bribing IOC members to earn votes. In 2001, Mormon business leader Mitt Romney (see page 106) was brought in to run the organizing committee for the Games, and he moved quickly to defuse the controversy.

The Games were considered a success in many ways, and they brought thousands of visitors to Salt Lake City, where thousands of volunteers, many Mormon, helped show off their city and their region. The Games earned a profit of nearly $100 million.

Strong on Faith and Family

Outsiders meeting Mormons for the first time might think of mysterious Church rituals closed to non-church members, or the old association with polygamy. Church leaders encourage others to see the Church of

Gold medal city
Looming behind the main LDS temple in Salt Lake City were these huge murals of cross-country skiers put up during the Winter Olympics in February, 2002. The Winter Games were seen as an important way to help Mormons spread word about their faith and culture to a worldwide audience.

Jesus Christ of Latter-day Saints as a truly Christian religion that inspires its members to be hardworking, law-abiding, and generous toward one another and their faith. In short, LDS president Hinckley wants outsiders to realize "We are not a weird people," as he told Mike Wallace on the television news show *60 Minutes* in December 2000.

Church leaders hope non-Mormons will notice the strengths of LDS life, such as the emphasis on family. Mormons set aside Monday evenings as family-only night; all busy schedules come to a halt to share a meal and perhaps scripture readings together. Strong church and family foundations may be why Utah's teen pregnancy rate is lower than the national average, and why so many LDS youth dedicate a year or two of service to their church before going on to marriage and families of their own.

As missionary Gavin Pouliot told the *Portsmouth Herald* in 2002, becoming a young adult "would've been harder if I hadn't grown up in the Church."

PIONEER DAY

For Latter-day Saints in Utah, there is a holiday that is like Christmas and the Fourth of July in one: Pioneer Day, celebrated each July 24. It marks the day in 1847 that Mormon pioneers first arrived at the barren valley of the Great Salt Lake. In 1897, the church threw a huge celebration to mark their 50th year in Utah, the completion of the Salt Lake Temple, and statehood for Utah.

Considering it their most important holiday, Mormons gather for parades, games, dances, feasting, and religious observances. Today, Pioneer Day is one of the biggest regional celebrations in North America.

5

The Mormon Church and Politics

AS THE MORMON CHURCH WAS FORMING, JOSEPH SMITH ADVISED his fledgling flock to obey the "laws of the land." But one concern for non-Mormons throughout the Church's history has been the extent to which the Mormons actually influence those laws. The Latter-day Saints, with much confidence in their faith and no inhibitions about expressing it, are a vocal group. And so their attraction to American politics is inevitable.

During their history the Mormons have affected politics on a variety of levels. In the Midwest they were a tight-knit sect on the run from local lawkeepers. In Utah, although hundreds of miles away from America's political center, their theocracy (rule by religious leaders) became such a huge success (and controversy) that their activities invoked the wrath of the top three levels of government: Congress, the presidency (who in turn called out the army at one point), and the Supreme Court. The Mormon way of life spurred federal legislation against it.

But the Latter-day Saints also wanted to be a part of America, and did what was necessary to lose their status as outcasts and enemies. Today, Latter-day Saints are comfortable insiders in the western United States. As the primary lawmakers of Utah, their domain has benefited financially and socially from their conservative and industrious approach to life. The prosperous, orderly landscape they have created continues to attract new non-Mormons, who now try to figure out how to fit in.

Church and Government as One

Smith called his new religion a "theo-democracy"—his goal was to create communities in which religious faith and government were one. Smith himself was most successful in Nauvoo, Illinois. As they would in Utah, the Mormons chose an almost unlivable place unwanted by others, a swamp on the Mississippi River, to begin creating God's kingdom on earth.

Enlisting his followers to build the kingdom quickly and efficiently, Smith amassed considerable power in just a few years. He was not only the head of their Church; he was head of Nauvoo's courts and city government, and bestowed upon himself the rank of general (complete with a military uniform) of Nauvoo's small army, the Nauvoo Legion. He even considered a run in the presidential campaign of 1844, but was murdered that summer (see page 21).

It was politics that first got Smith's foot in the door—Illinois politicians vying for Mormon votes gave Smith unusually broad powers in his city-state of Nauvoo. Then, it was reaction to Smith's combination of church and city policies that caused the Mormons' eviction from Illinois. When a local newspaper publisher wrote anti-Mormon tracts, he discovered he was breaking Smith's Nauvoo laws and his press was destroyed. Non-Mormons, however, did not sympathize with Smith ignoring the First Amendment (which guarantees freedom of the press), and when polygamy was added to the mix, the Mormons were violently expelled from Nauvoo.

A Would-Be Empire

Once in Utah, 800 miles from the nearest settled American community, Brigham Young felt safe putting a theocracy into place, and he did it in a grand way. As the first white settlers in this new territory, a prize won from the Mexican War, the Mormons had no competing governments or local community standards to bump up against.

Young envisioned a mini-empire called Deseret, a word from the Book of Mormon meaning honeybee. As he saw it, Deseret would stretch southwest as far as San Diego in California, and reach up into Oregon and Wyoming.

PRECEDING PAGE
Asking for votes
Utah senator Orrin Hatch, seen here in 1999 during his brief run for the presidency.

From their first settlement at Salt Lake City, Mormons fanned out through Deseret and formed new communities, according to Young's direction and assignments. The short-lived Deseret area was renamed the Utah Territory in 1850 by the federal government, and Young was named its governor.

Young always intended for Deseret to be a part of the United States, and did not set out to be a disruptive force in the West. He was perhaps just unrealistic about the level of self-control and independence the U.S. government would tolerate from a territory settlement. To help the Utah area grow and to remain self-reliant, the Mormons developed a variety of industries, such silk, cotton, paper, and sugar, that employed the new Mormon pioneers streaming into the Salt Lake Basin.

But it was not just Mormon converts who were heading West. The building of Deseret coincided with the discovery of gold in California in 1848. A growing number of westward settlers, on their way to pan for gold, decided to go no further than Utah. Arriving there, they discovered that the Mormon settlements were relatively peaceful and stable—Salt Lake City had no need for a jail until its non-Mormon population increased significantly.

Soon, however, complaints began making their way to Washington, D.C., about the LDS Church excluding non-church members from sharing in Utah's prosperity. "Those that do not like our looks and our customs are at liberty to go where they please. But if they remain with us, they must obey the laws sanctioned by us," Young said (as quoted in *Journal of Discourses*, a collection of Brigham Young's writings).

The shocking announcement of polygamy came in 1852 (see chapter 4), and over the next few years non-Mormons reported use of a strange language among some Utah settlers. The always-enterprising Mormons were dabbling with the English language, trying to make it easier for non-English-speaking new Church members, but to outsiders it sounded decidedly un-American.

A War of Words and Legislation

The Republican Party was formed in 1854 and included among its goals the promise to eradicate polygamy from the American landscape—a direct reference to the practice of the Latter-day Saints. By 1856 there were 22,000 Mormons in the Salt Lake Basin, and the U.S. government finally considered them threatening enough to be declared by President James Buchanan in a state of "rebellion." In 1857 troops headed for Utah to unseat territory governor Young.

In the ensuing Utah War with the federal government, no Mormons were killed, beaten or driven from their homes, as they had been in Missouri or Illinois years earlier. Rather, the federal government used law, and the threat of armed conflict (a U.S. Army base was established just south of Salt Lake City) to try to force the Latter-day Saints to conform to mainstream American life.

The Mormons' struggle with the federal government lasted 30 years. By 1860 the territory's population had grown to 50,000; in another 20 years it was 144,000, most of whom were Mormons. During that time governors and judges were appointed by the federal government in an attempt to diminish Mormon political power.

Defeated by 'the Principle'

The Mormons were unbeatable financially, with their self-sufficient communities and commercial loyalty to Mormon-run businesses. But as it turned out, they gave their political enemies an easy target with polygamy. The controversy made it to the capitol building in Washington, D.C., where Congress passed an anti-polygamy law in 1862, signed by President Abraham Lincoln. The Civil War and its aftermath gave the Mormons a breather from government pressure, but only temporarily.

When polygamous Mormons hid their plural marriages, they were arrested under new federal laws prohibiting cohabitation (living together without being married). Even Young was convicted of "lewd and lascivious cohabitation" and served an in-home prison sentence. The conviction of Young's secretary, George Reynolds, provided the Mormons with a polygamy case they could use to test the law. They fought his conviction up to the Supreme Court. The case was settled in 1879, two years after Young's death. Yes, the court ruled, it was permissible to treat polygamy as a punishable offense.

"I defy the United States. I will obey God," declared John Taylor (1808–1887), Young's successor as Church president and prophet. In response, an 1882 law withheld the privileges of voting and serving in an elected office from anyone convicted of polygamy or cohabitation. Hundreds of Mormon men in plural marriages were imprisoned or forced

into hiding. Women were jailed for refusing to testify against their husbands because the courts did not recognize their marriage.

The next round in the legal battle between Mormons and the federal government, the Edmunds-Tucker Act of 1887, was crippling to the Mormon Church. Adultery (sex outside of marriage) was declared a felony (another way of prosecuting polygamists), as was performing a marriage that was not recorded publicly. The Edmunds-Tucker Act also gave government the right to seize church property worth more than $50,000, and the Mormons were forced to rent their Salt Lake City tabernacle from the federal government. Mormon schools were closed and funds set aside to help emigrating Church members were confiscated. LDS president Taylor remained defiant. From his hiding place in Davis County, Utah, he encouraged Mormons to remain faithful before he died that year.

Under the temporary leadership of the Twelve Apostles, discussion grew of giving up "the Principle." Latter-day Saints lobbyists in Washington reported back that statehood for Utah, something the Mormon Church was eager to attain, would never be granted as long as polygamy remained a Mormon practice. Meanwhile, the Supreme Court upheld Edmunds-Tucker, calling the Mormons openly rebellious against the U.S. government. Church leaders, the court believed, held "absolute ecclesiastical [church-based] control" of its membership. Encouraged by the court's decision, Congress was considering revoking the U.S. citizenship of Mormon Church members.

The Mormons Enter a New Era

The Mormons, with their leaders in jail or in hiding and even their plural wives on the run, were backed into a corner. Wilford Woodruff, from whose wagon Young first set eyes on the Great Salt Lake Valley 40 years earlier, assumed the Church presidency at age 82 in 1889.

The Mormons attempted some goodwill gestures, as when hundreds of polygamous men turned themselves in for lighter sentences, while Elliot Sanford, a judge sympathetic to the Church, sat on the territory's supreme court. Woodruff also ordered destruction of the Endowment House, where plural marriages were secretly performed. But these gestures were not enough. Sanford was replaced by a tougher judge at the end of 1889. Woodruff had difficult decisions to make.

The LDS Church was entering a new era, said an official Church statement. No longer would it seek control of Utah by controlling its thousands of Church members. In 1890 came another statement: Mormons should refrain from entering into new plural marriages, a Manifesto tearfully approved by the Quorum of the Twelve Apostles.

In 1891 the Church suggested that Utah residents abolish the pro- and anti-Mormon political parties and align themselves with the national Democrat or Republican parties. Woodruff also abolished the

Council of Fifty (one of the LDS Church's early leadership bodies). Over a period of a few years Woodruff dismantled the 60-year-old theocracy that Smith and Young had taught was God's will for America.

Woodruff's policies were effective. By 1894 President Benjamin Harrison offered "full amnesty and pardon" to those whose plural marriages began before 1890's Manifesto. Rights to vote or hold political office in the territory were restored to all Utah residents. On January 4, 1896, the Mormon-owned *Deseret News* reported that, on its seventh attempt, the territory of Utah was now the state of Utah.

Important revelation

In 1890, LDS president Wilford Woodruff announced that he had received a new revelation from God that said polygamy was no longer to be practiced by members of the Church.

Some Mormons never accepted this meeker version of their church—with no more Mormon militia or political parties, and no more polygamy. Just as Taylor shook his fist at the federal government, thousands of former Mormons in the Salt Lake Basin area still defy the government and the LDS Church as they continue to abide by "the Principle."

The Latter-day Saints changed their course in the 1890s when they sacrificed not only polygamy but the entire ideal of building Zion in America. By joining America instead of trying to recreate it, they went from being a radical, outlaw church to a conservative one with its own place in the American landscape.

Since Utah's statehood the Mormons have claimed "non-interference of Church authority in political matters" (as stated by the office of Church president Joseph F. Smith in 1907) and that "the Church does not become involved in politics," as LDS president Gordon Hinckley told Larry King on CNN in 1998. But in reality the LDS Church still exerts much influence in Utah and, when it can, beyond. Still well-organized and extremely well-funded, the LDS Church seems to find politics not only affirming but irresistible.

Joining the National Political Scene

Just as George Ryan's polygamy conviction was a Mormon legal test case in the 1870s, Reed Smoot's candidacy for the United States Senate early in the 20th century served as a political test case for the Mormons, eager to contribute to national politics. Smoot (see page 102) was a Church Apostle elected to the U.S. Senate in 1902. His challenge as a Mormon was not winning an election, but actually taking his seat in the Senate.

Smoot did not practice polygamy, so he was grilled by other Senators about Church finances, asking whether the Mormon Church was not really just a business empire designed to make its leaders wealthy through business enterprises and tithing. Church president Joseph F. Smith, the founder's nephew, was called to testify and restate the Church's position on polygamy.

In the end, with support from President Theodore Roosevelt, Smoot took his place in the Senate in 1906. Smoot represented Utah as a conservative Republican for 30 years, eventually becoming chairman of the important Senate Finance Committee. More important for the LDS Church, he normalized the idea of Mormons participating in the national political scene. In 1932 he and many other Republicans lost their Congressional seats in a Democratic landslide led by Franklin D. Roosevelt. Toward the end of Smoot's Senate tenure, another Mormon, J. Reuben Clark (1871–1961), was named ambassador to Mexico, a position he held for three years before becoming a First Counselor to the Church president when Democrats took over the White House.

Smoot (see page 102)

A SUCCESS STORY

Ivy Baker Priest, treasury secretary under President Dwight Eisenhower in the 1950s and treasurer of California when Ronald Reagan was governor in the 1960s, grew up the daughter of a poor miner in Bingham, Utah. In Washington, D.C., she learned to mingle with the rich and powerful.

A story told on the web site www.onlineutah.com's history section points to Priest's skills. At one dinner she was seated next to popular minister and successful author Norman Vincent Peale (1898–1993). Peale told Priest that most successful people he met had had an obstacle to overcome, and he wondered if she did, too. "Poverty," was her immediate reply. "And now," Peale said with a laugh, "you're in charge of all that money!"

Achieving Top Positions in Washington

By the 1950s Mormons were turning up more frequently in national office. Ivy Baker Priest (1905–1975) served as treasury secretary under Republican president Dwight Eisenhower (see the box on page 91). Ezra Taft Benson (see page 102) was a Mormon Church Apostle during his tenure as Eisenhower's agriculture secretary, and went on to become Church president and prophet, as well.

In the 1960s Democratic president John Kennedy tapped Mormon congressman Stewart Udall from Arizona, whose father had been the state's Supreme Court chief justice, to be interior secretary—a position Udall kept when Lyndon Johnson assumed the presidency. Udall then had an opportunity to be influential in one of his favorite causes—the environment (see the box on page 93). At the end of the decade, with Republicans back in the White House, David Matthew Kennedy (1905–1996) was President Richard Nixon's treasury secretary.

Church member Gregory J. Newell (b.1949) served in a high-level advisory position to President Ronald Reagan before he was appointed to the State Department, then to the ambassadorship to Sweden. George Romney (see page 105) was secretary of Housing and Urban Development under Nixon, and later governor of Michigan. Brent Scowcroft (b.1925) served as national security advisor to President Gerald Ford and the first President George Bush.

Flourishing in a Conservative Era

Mormon politics flourished in the socially conservative era ushered in by Reagan's election as president in 1980. The Mormons had a lot of company (such as the Christian-based Moral Majority) in their conservative stands on social issues such as abortion and the Equal Rights Amendment (ERA) for women. In speaking out on social issues in the last quarter of the 20th century, the Mormon Church became more assertive in its political activism.

One hundred years earlier, Mormon women who enjoyed voting rights in local elections were active in the movement for national women's suffrage (the right to vote). Susan B. Anthony (1820–1906), a 19th-century feminist whose primary focus was voting rights for women, was a popular speaker in Utah.

But even then female Mormons were conservative about other women's issues: When another feminist in that era, Elizabeth Cady

A Mormon Political Family

Although the typical Mormon in government is Republican, two Latter-day Saints who excelled in the art of national politics as Democrats were Arizona brothers Stewart Udall (b.1920) and Morris "Mo" Udall (1922–1998, pictured). Their ancestors were an English couple who came to America with thousands of other English Mormon converts in Utah's early days. Their grandparents were prominent Mormon leaders in Arizona, and their father was Arizona Supreme Court justice Levi Stewart Udall (1891–1960).

Mo Udall spent 30 years as an Arizona congressman and unsuccessfully ran for the presidency in 1976. He embraced traditional Democratic causes such as environmental protection, and was the first prominent Democrat to oppose President Lyndon Johnson's decision to increase U.S. involvement in the Vietnam War.

Renowned for his sense of humor and admired for his ability to rise above partisan politics, he counted among his close friends Arizona's conservative Republican senator Barry Goldwater.

Stewart Udall also served in Congress, which he left when appointed secretary of the interior by President John Kennedy. He continued in that position under President Johnson. Like his brother Mo, Stewart Udall was an advocate for environmental protection, and had his hand in a number of conservation laws, including the Wilderness Act.

Stewart Udall left Washington and returned to the Southwest to practice law and write. But his quiet life was interrupted in 1978 when he was asked to visit communities located downwind of the Nevada Test Site, whose residents were experiencing a high rate of cancer. Udall spent 12 years pushing the federal government to compensate citizens exposed to radiation from atomic tests.

He wrote a book in 2002, *The Forgotten Founders: Rethinking the History of the Old West,* about unsung heroes in the formation of his beloved American West. His son Tom Udall (b.1948) carries on the family tradition, having served in Congress as a representative from New Mexico since 1999.

Speaking her mind
Pro-ERA activist Sonia Johnson (at left in this photo) was excommunicated from the LDS Church because of her support for the Equal Rights Amendment.

Stanton (1815–1902), came to Salt Lake City to speak about birth control, she was not well received. Voting rights would enable women to help build the kingdom of God, while birth control was contrary to it.

In the 20th century, the Mormon Church called upon its members to oppose ratification of the ERA in 1978, because they believed it would have a negative effect on the sanctity of women. Most LDS women did oppose the amendment. Some who did not paid a high price, such as lifelong church member and housewife-turned-activist Sonia Johnson (b.1936). She criticized the Church's policy of using Church funds to influence members' votes on various issues, such as the ERA. Johnson's support of the ERA resulted in her being excommunicated, or removed, from the LDS Church in 1979.

In 1980 Mormon Church member Paula Hawkins (b.1927) was the first woman elected to the U.S. Senate from Florida. She ran a campaign compatible with Church teachings, calling herself the "Maitland (Florida) Housewife" who would relate to ordinary folk. She proved to be an effective force in government, especially in the areas of child abuse prevention and programs to treat women struggling with substance abuse.

Lingering Anti-Mormon Prejudice

Despite what seems today to be universal acceptance of Mormons in every level of government inside and outside of Utah, some of the old political battle cries can still be heard occasionally. Matt Salmon, an LDS candidate for governor of Arizona in 2002, was distressed when "Vote Mormon" signs popped up in yards of homeowners who supported other candidates. The simple message reinforced the stereotype of Mormon voting blocks in single-minded pursuit of political power. However, Salmon recalled the Mormons' theocracy days when he appeared on a Christian television program and spoke of the need for religious people to "reclaim" government.

A few years earlier, across the country in Massachusetts, Republican Mitt Romney attempted to unseat the state's longtime senator, Ted Kennedy. Kennedy's nephew, Congressman Joe Kennedy, brought up Romney's LDS membership in an attempt at negative campaigning: He pointed out that the LDS Church, until recently, banned African Americans from the position of priesthood, and the Church's Book of Mormon claimed dark-skinned people would forever be in God's disfavor. Romney pointed out the obvious irony of a Kennedy using religion as a negative campaign device, since it was Kennedy's brother, John F. Kennedy, who had experienced prejudice against his Catholic faith while barely winning the 1960 presidential election. Although defeated in the senate race, Romney went on to a successful campaign to become the state's governor in 2002.

Most Comfortable as Republicans

There were 16 LDS members in the 107th Congress, seated in 2000, most of them from western states. Among those 16, 12 were Republican, the party that LDS politicians have aligned themselves with most frequently. One Mormon who ran unsuccessfully for Congress as a Utah Democrat in the 2002 elections, Dave Thomas, said that LDS teachings are actually more compatible with Democratic traditions. Thomas, for example, favors clear separation of church and state.

Respected Mormon author Eugene England (1933–2001) would have agreed with Thomas. Shortly before his death, England scolded Utah Democrats for their consistently weak showing on election days. After all, he claimed, successful East Coast Mormon political candidates tend to be Democrats, the party that is more closely linked to social programs helpful to the downtrodden and, therefore, more

High Office

Mike Leavitt is sworn in for his second term as governor of Utah in 1997. A member of the Latter-day Saints, Leavitt is one of a majority of Mormons holding high offices in the state.

actively Christian. As the demographics in Utah continue to slowly slide in favor of non-Mormons, the term "Democratic Mormon" may cease to be an oxymoron. But while the majority of the ever-growing Mormon Church membership continues to favor conservative issues, it will most likely be the Republican party that claims their effective support.

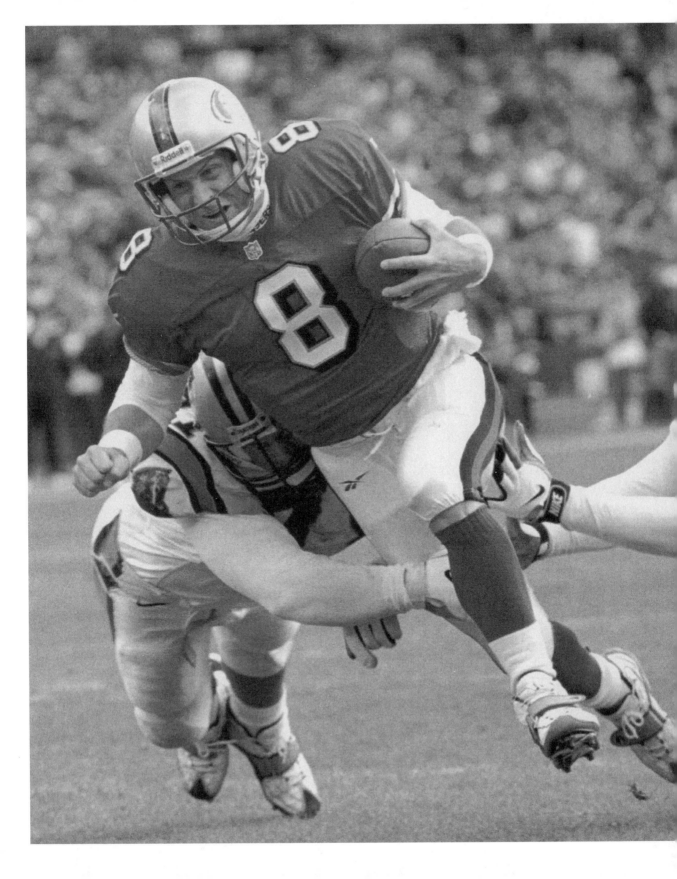

6

Prominent Mormon Americans

FROM JOSEPH SMITH TO MITT ROMNEY, FROM BRIGHAM YOUNG TO Steve Young, Mormons have played key roles in American history and culture. Many leaders and prominent members of the LDS Church have been influential or visible in American society. Mormons often bring their distinct religious values to their work and play, but also blend into mainstream American life as typical citizens. This chapter describes a few of the most visible Mormons in American history—people who have influenced the Church and the nation. (The events of the lives of Mormon founder Joseph Smith and his key successor, Brigham Young, are covered in the introduction and in chapters 1 and 2.)

Jonathan Browning (? –1879) and
John Moses Browning (1855–1926)

Jonathan Browning was a gunsmith from Tennessee who moved to Quincy, Illinois, in 1834 and gained fame for inventing a repeating rifle (a long gun that can be fired more than once without reloading). When the Mormons arrived in Illinois from Missouri in 1839, Browning was curious and went to meet Joseph Smith. He and his wife converted to the Mormon faith in 1842 and moved to Nauvoo, impressed by the community's devotion.

Browning's arrival came at a crucial time, when Illinois had revoked Nauvoo citizen's rights to purchase arms due to conflicts between Mormons and outsiders. Browning built a gun shop attached to his home in Nauvoo and made firearms; his Nauvoo guns had an engraved plate on each one reading, "Holiness to the Lord—Our Preservation."

When mobs drove the Mormons from Nauvoo in 1846 (see page 33), Browning closed shop and crossed the Mississippi River, where Brigham Young asked him to make guns for the migrating pioneers. Browning made 400 firearms, staying in Iowa to outfit Mormons for their journey West. Browning guns were well used on the plains for defense and to shoot game.

In 1852 Browning was asked to lead a pioneer group to Utah, and he started a gunsmithing business in Ogden, Utah, soon after he arrived. He died in 1879.

His son John Moses Browning worked in the gun shop and made his first gun at age 13. He and his brothers founded the Browning Arms Company, which still makes guns today. The younger Browning patented a single-shot rifle in 1879 and formed a partnership with the Winchester Company in 1883 that pioneered the most popular guns in American history. He later invented the automatic machine gun or "Browning Peacemaker" first used in the Spanish-American War (1898), and made U.S. military sidearms that were used for almost 75 years. His weapons played a prominent role in World War I and World War II; the pistol that assassinated Archduke Franz Ferdinand in 1914 and sparked World War I was a Browning.

John Browning owned more than 120 patents for new firearms. Browning Arms, still located in northern Utah, celebrated its 125th anniversary in 2003.

Emmeline B. Wells (1828–1921)

This petite woman was a nationally-known feminist, writer, editor, businesswoman, and president of the LDS Relief Society (1910–1921). She led the women of the Church and traveled across the West. She also led a mission to store wheat and sold 200,000 bushels to the U.S. government for relief efforts in Europe during World War I.

Wells edited and published an independent LDS feminist newspaper from 1877 to 1914, known as the *Woman's Exponent*. She was wife number seven of a polygamous man, yet was also a tireless advocate

PRECEDING PAGE
Top quarterback
Steve Young is one of the top quarterbacks in National Football League history. A graduate of BYU and a relative of Brigham Young, Steve Young is a practicing Mormon and one of the most well-known members of the faith nationwide.

for women's rights—including the rights to vote, work outside the home, hold public positions or political office, and pursue any career. A suffragette and "woman's rights woman," Emmeline traveled across the country speaking and working with well-known American feminists Susan B. Anthony and Elizabeth Cady Stanton.

Wells was a symbol of Mormon women's power, as well as their loss of power at the turn of the 19th century. In 1921, she became the first Relief Society president to be released from her duties. Previously, all Society presidents held their office until death, as did male Church

Woman's rights advocate
Emmeline Wells was president of the LDS Relief Society and an important writer, editor, and activist in the late 19th and early 20th centuries.

presents. LDS president Heber J. Grant let Wells go in 1921—in a move many believed was aimed at curbing female power in the Church. The shock of dismissal wounded Wells so deeply that she died not long after.

Reed Smoot (1862–1941)

In 1902, Reed Smoot became the first Mormon elected to the U.S. Senate, representing Utah as a member of the Republican Party. This made him the highest-ranking Mormon in federal government and fulfilled the Church's goal of putting an Apostle (important Church leader) in the U.S. Congress. However, Smoot's election proved to be controversial for the Mormons and the state of Utah.

A Mormon and a monogamist, Smoot was accused of presenting a false image of Utah as being monogamist while covering up polygamy among high-ranking Mormons who still practiced it. The Salt Lake Ministerial Association launched a campaign to expose the newly-elected Smoot as a secret supporter of polygamy, charging that he had taken a secret pledge of disloyalty to the American government. A Senate committee conducted hearings to investigate Smoot and questioned his ability to serve in the U.S. Senate, regarding his testimony on polygamy as dishonest and hypocritical. In early 1903, they voted to expel Smoot, but with President Theodore Roosevelt's support, the Senate finally allowed Smoot to take his seat later in 1903.

He served for 30 years, until he was defeated during a Democratic Party landslide led by President Franklin D. Roosevelt in 1932.

Ezra Taft Benson (1899–1994)

Benson was the 13th prophet and president of the LDS Church and later the first Mormon to hold a Cabinet post in the federal government. A farmer from Idaho known for his ultra-conservative political views and affinity for the John Birch Society (an ultraconservative political organization that supported what many people believed to be racist and anti-semitic views), Benson believed America's founding fathers were inspired by God in establishing the U.S. Constitution and government. He believed the United States was "a chosen nation" of God, who made it a free country destined for the Mormon restoration of the Gospel. Benson devoted his life to the dual responsibilities of church and nation.

Benson was called to served as an Apostle of the LDS Church in 1943. During and after World War II, he helped coordinate relief efforts

for European countries. In 1953, President Dwight Eisenhower named Benson to serve as secretary of agriculture, and he did so until 1961.

When Benson became prophet in 1985, he was less vocal about his politics and well-liked by most members of the Church. He continued to preach conservative values, such as full-time motherhood and discouraging birth control and work outside of the home for women. Benson avidly supported Presidents Ronald Reagan and George H.W. Bush, as well as conservative politics in general. Benson's career in public life helped influence Mormons to become more politically active and form conservative coalitions (see chapter 5).

J. Willard Marriott (1900–1985)

This devout Mormon was the founder and chairman of the Marriott Corporation, an international hotel and restaurant company. Marriott began his career at age 13 on his father's Utah farm, enlisting his siblings to raise a lettuce crop, which he sold for $2,000, giving the money to his father. He then sold sheep and woolen goods, building up a sales force of 45 college students selling in seven states. He even sold woolen underwear to lumberjacks in the Pacific Northwest.

Marriott worked to put himself through college at the University of Utah; many years later, after his success in business, he funded the school's Marriott Library. After serving a Mormon mission in New England, Marriott launched his restaurant career with a small A&W Root Beer store in Washington, D.C., in 1927.

Marriott went on to create the Marriott Hotel chain, a business with more than $600 million in annual revenue. Marriott restaurants grew into a worldwide food business supplying airlines and colleges with meals. The company's hotel chains now include Marriott, Ritz-Carlton, Ramada, Courtyard, Residence Inn, and others.

Marriott's keys to success were a global outlook, good service, and quality products. He also credited his Mormon faith with giving him traditional values of hard work and honesty. He held leadership positions in the LDS Church, and placed a copy of the Book of Mormon in all Marriott hotels in the drawer next to a Bible traditionally supplied by the Gideon organization.

In 1972, Marriott's son, J. Willard "Bill" Marriott, Jr. (b.1932), became Marriott CEO. On the company's web site (www.marriott.com), the elder Marriott is quoted as saying, "America is the land of unlimited opportunities for those who will pay the price . . . . A man should keep on being constructive, and make every day count, to the very end."

Esther Eggertsen Peterson (190?–1994)

This prominent activist and feminist was an advocate for women, workers, and consumers across America and around the world. Born in Provo, Utah, she graduated from Brigham Young University and earned a master's degree from Columbia University in New York. She was an educator, lobbyist, government official, corporate executive, and advocate for the rights of working women and men. In 1938, Peterson became a union organizer, and during World War II she worked to integrate African-American women into unions. Peterson also worked to raise the minimum wage in America.

In 1961, President John F. Kennedy appointed her assistant secretary of labor and director of the Women's Bureau. She launched "equal pay for equal work" legislation (aimed at making sure women got paid the same as men for doing the same jobs) and led the first President's Commission on the Status of Women.

Under Presidents Lyndon B. Johnson and Jimmy Carter, she was the special assistant for consumer affairs and secured "truth in packaging" laws for food products that required them to list all ingredients. In 1981, her work to protect American consumers helped her earn the Presidential Medal of Freedom, the nation's highest civilian award.

In 1993, President Bill Clinton named her a delegate to the United Nations General Assembly at age 87, where she worked with UNESCO as an advocate for the needs of working Americans.

George W. Romney (1907–1995)

George Romney was the chairman and president of American Motors Corporation (AMC) from 1954 to 1962 and later a prominent national politician. Romney saved AMC from collapse by dropping the Nash and Hudson cars in 1957 in favor of a compact Rambler model. AMC's sales quadrupled in two years, and Rambler became the third best-selling car in America. Romney's idea of a compact automobile was ahead of his time, bringing the economy car to Americans.

Moving into politics, Romney was elected to three terms as governor of Michigan, urging civil rights and tax reform. Following the dictates of the LDS Church, Romney never smoked or drank alcohol. He also served as a Mormon missionary and gave 10 percent of his income to the Church, which he later served in the local office of bishop.

Romney brought the Mormon faith into the national spotlight when he ran for president in 1968 and his religion became an issue. Observers wondered if the Mormon faith would influence Romney's candidacy. However, Romney dropped out of the race after he stunned fellow Republicans by candidly admitting on television that his support for the Vietnam War was due to being "brainwashed" by the U.S. military. He later repeatedly called U.S. participation in the war "the most tragic foreign policy mistake in the nation's history."

Romney went on to serve as secretary of Housing and Urban Development (HUD) from 1969 to 1973 in President Richard Nixon's cabinet, but he left because support for urban programs was less than he had hoped for. In 1974, he founded the National Volunteer Center, which merged with the Points of Light Foundation in 1991.

Mitt Romney

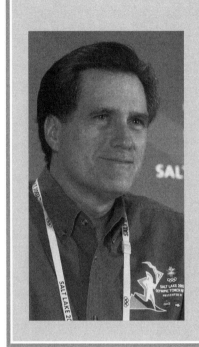

Businessman Mitt Romney (b.1947) followed in his father's footsteps as a national figure in business and public life. After graduating from BYU and earning business and law degrees from Harvard University, the younger Romney became a successful investor. He founded Bain Capital in 1984, a firm that invests in hundreds of companies. He also co-founded the Staples Office Supply chain. In 1994, Romney ran for the U.S. Senate in Massachusetts, but lost to Senator Ted Kennedy.

In 1999, at age 52, Romney was recruited to be the CEO of the Salt Lake 2002 Olympic Winter Games, to reverse the group's shaky image after an Olympic bribery scandal. His business success continued, as the Games turned a profit of more than $100 million—one of the most successful Winter Olympics ever.

In November 2002, Mitt Romney became the first Mormon to be elected governor of Massachusetts, following in his father's gubernatorial footsteps. As a bonus, in 2002, *People* magazine chose him as one of America's 50 most beautiful people.

Orrin Hatch (b.1934)

This Republican senator from Utah was first elected to the U.S. Senate in 1976. Orrin Hatch is a powerful senior senator and chairman of the Senate Judiciary Committee. A graduate of BYU and a practicing Mormon, Hatch's views often oppose liberal and feminist agendas.

His aggressive questioning of Professor Anita Hill in the 1991 Senate hearings to confirm Clarence Thomas for the Supreme Court outraged feminists. Hatch had similarly interrogated Sonia Johnson (see page 94) during her testimony supporting the Equal Rights Amendment. He wanted to impeach President Bill Clinton, yet offered forgiveness if Clinton would confess what he had done.

Hatch embodies Mormon values in his politics, yet says he does not take direction from Church leaders. He is a staunch defender of freedom of religion, even religious cults.

Hatch opposes abortion rights, yet he supports birth control and occasionally sides with liberal Democratic senator Ted Kennedy. He has six children and is a grandfather, writes song lyrics, and has recorded four albums (see the box on page 108), including one with Gladys Knight. Hatch ran for president in 2000 but did not make it past the primaries.

Merlin Olsen (b.1940)

This Mormon football player gained popularity and visibility as a college and National Football League superstar in the 1960s and 1970s. Merlin Olsen played football for Utah State University, where he was named All-America and earned the Outland Trophy as the nation's top lineman. Joining the Los Angeles Rams in 1962, he became part of one of the most famous defensive lines in NFL history, the "Fearsome Foursome."

Olsen was selected to the Pro Bowl, the NFL's annual all-star game, 14 years in a row—more than any other player in history. In 1982, he was elected to the Pro Football Hall of Fame, and in 1994 was named to the league's 75th anniversary all-time team.

Following his pro football career, Olsen became a sports broadcaster, and also appeared as an actor in many movies and television shows. His most prominent roles were as Father Murphy on *Little House on the Prairie* and another show named for his character. He also was a longtime spokesman for the FTD flower-delivery company.

Donny (b.1958) and Marie (b.1960) Osmond

Perhaps the most recognizable Mormons in America today are singers and entertainers Donny and Marie Osmond. They are part of a singing family that at one time was among the most popular singing groups in the country.

The Osmonds were an established group when Donny and Marie were paired for the first time in 1973. They released six top-selling albums in the next four years. When they co-hosted *The Mike Douglas Show* in 1975, they were such a hit that ABC offered them their own variety show. In 1976, Donny (then 18) and Marie (then 16) became the youngest hosts of a weekly prime-time TV variety show. *The Donny & Marie Show* aired every Friday night from 1976 to 1979, winning millions of fans and earning a People's Choice Award in 1979 for favorite variety show.

Donny and Marie's smiling, wholesome faces, silly antics, sibling rivalry, and talent made them megastars and household names.

After the show ended, they continued to perform together in concerts until 1986, then went on to pursue solo careers as entertainers. Marie returned to country music and had a number of hits, while Donny went to perform on Broadway in 1982 in the musical *Little Johnny Jones*.

They both struggled in the 1980s and early 1990s to find themselves and work through personal issues. Donny had problems with anxiety and fear, and Marie suffered severe depression. Yet they both overcame personal difficulties to maintain an energetic presence in American culture. Donny returned to the Top 40 in 1989 with "Soldier of Love" and two more albums. He starred on Broadway in 1992 in *Joseph and the Amazing Technicolor Dreamcoat*, which ran for more than five years. Marie appeared on stage as well, starring in *The Sound of Music* and *The King and I*.

In 1998, the duo returned to television with a talk show, *Donny & Marie*, which was nominated for five daytime Emmys in 2000. Donny published his autobiography, *Life Is Just What You Make It— My Story*,

Songwriting Senator

Politics is not everything to Orrin Hatch. In his Washington office Hatch has a large antique cabinet full of compact discs, all featuring songs written by him. Hatch took up songwriting in 1996 and has enjoyed some success. His song "Little Angel of Mine" was on the soundtrack of the 2002 movie *Stuart Little 2*.

Many of his songs are inspirational or patriotic, such as "My God Is Love" and "Heal Our Land." His CD released in 2002, *I Love America*, features "America United," a song he wrote just after the September 11, 2001, terrorist attacks.

His Mormon faith may give him an occasional advantage in the songwriting industry—one of his songs was featured on the soundtrack for the film *Joshua*, about a Mormon missionary. But otherwise Hatch's faith can work against his commercial success—marketing his inspirational music is tough because there is a fairly large bias in the Christian music market against Mormons, he told a reporter for the *Christian Science Monitor* in 2002.

in 1999. When Donny and Marie hosted the Miss America Pageant in 1999, Donny thrilled the audience with a charismatic comeback, and Marie made pageant history by being the first woman to announce the new Miss America. They hosted the pageant again in October 2000.

Steven R. Covey, (b.1932)

Steven Covey is one of the best-selling authors in America. His 1989 book *The 7 Habits of Highly Effective People* was a *New York Times* number-one best seller and has sold more than 12 million copies in 32 languages in 70 countries. It was called "the most influential business book of the 20th Century" by *Chief Executive* magazine in 1997.

Covey's seven steps to success have made him an American business guru, and he is eagerly sought for consulting, speeches, seminars, and coaching. Covey has taught leadership principles and management skills for more than 25 years in business, government, and education. His ideas have been adopted by thousands of organizations. His book launched a dozen more books on the same 7 Habits theme, and he has written two other books, *First Things First* and *Principle-Centered Leadership*. He also launched a magazine, *Executive Excellence*, in 1995.

Covey holds an MBA from Harvard University and a Ph.D. from BYU, where he was professor of organizational behavior and business management. He founded Covey Leadership Center and The Institute for Principle Centered Leadership, dedicated to assisting education and community life.

In 1996, Covey merged with Franklin Quest to form Franklin-Covey Co., a 4,500-member international firm seeking to inspire positive change in the habits, methods, and practices of people and organizations. FranklinCovey clients include America's largest companies, thousands of smaller companies, and government at all levels. Franklin-Covey works with cities to transform communities, and teaches the 7 Habits in more than 3,500 school districts and universities nationwide and to education leaders in 27 states. FranklinCovey products, such as business diaries, notebooks, and organizational charts, are used by more than 15 million people worldwide.

Steve Young (b.1961)

Steve Young is among the most successful college and professional football quarterbacks of all time. Young played football for BYU, the Tampa

Bay Buccaneers, and was the star quarterback of the San Francisco 49ers from 1987 to 1999. He is among the NFL's all-time leaders in passer rating, a measurement of passing success for quarterbacks.

At BYU, Young was named All-America in 1983, while setting numerous records including one for the highest single-season pass com-

Media Stars of Generation Y

Some fresh new faces in the media at the start of the 21st century belong to young Mormon women, who keep the faith while surfing a hyper-modern culture. Julie Stoffer of MTV's *Real World,* Neleh Dennis of *Survivor*, Eliza Dushku of *Buffy the Vampire Slayer* (pictured), and the musical group SHeDAISY all offer the American public a look at the LDS Church's young women. These girls are diverse and unique; most are practicing Mormons. Each woman has emerged from Mormon tradition to take a visible role in American pop culture.

Stoffer, a BYU student, was expelled from the Mormon school for violating its "honor code" when she shared a house with men and women on MTV's *Real World* in 2000. She struggled with her Mormon upbringing on camera and chose freedom and self-discovery rather than obedience to BYU standards. In the process, Stoffer became an accidental role model for thousands of Mormon women.

Dennis, a 21-year-old student from Utah, appeared on *Survivor: Marquesas* and brought along the LDS scriptures as her luxury item. She survived to the bitter end, as the second-place finalist. Dennis is a dancer, singer, actor, certified nurse assistant, psychology major, scuba diver, and lifeguard.

Dushku, an actress of Scandinavian-Albanian descent from Boston, plays a "bad" character named Faith on the television series *Buffy the Vampire Slayer*. Dushku's Mormon relatives are appalled by her character's immoral behavior, yet she enjoys exploring a dark persona in her work. She does have some family support. Dushku said her mother is a person who "loves strong women who hold their own. She's always rooted for me and all women in the business to make a difference," (as quoted in an April 23, 1999, article by Michelle Green on www.anotheruniverse.com).

The musical group known as SHeDAISY, three Mormon sisters from Magna, Utah, have come a long way from singing in church, but they say their parents and the Gospel gave them their foundation.

Kristyn Osborn of the group said on their web site (www.shedaisy.com), "We're just very grateful for this opportunity to have the chance to be doing this. We believe strongly that there is a purpose. We just try to be mindful of that and rely on the basic principles of the Gospel for our big decisions and strengths."

pletion percentage in college football history. He was the runner-up in voting for the Heisman Trophy, given to college football's top player.

Young was drafted by the Tampa Bay Buccaneers as the first pick of the 1984 NFL draft, but he struggled with the young and inexperienced team. In 1991, Young joined the San Francisco 49ers, where he briefly backed up superstar quarterback Joe Montana. Young emerged from Montana's shadow in 1992, earning NFL Player of the Year honors and setting an all-time record with a 112.8 passer rating for the season.

He went on to become the only quarterback to lead the league in passing four straight years (1991–1994), and led the 49ers to two Super Bowl championships. In Super Bowl XXIX, he threw a record six touchdown passes in the team's 49–21 rout of the Denver Broncos. By the time he retired after the 2000 season, Young had the highest career passer rating at 96.8, and had thrown 232 touchdown passes.

Young is the great-great-great-grandson of Brigham Young and a church-attending, devout Latter-day Saint. While still playing in the NFL, he earned a law degree from BYU, and became a popular speaker across the country. He lends his visibility to sports causes as well as appearing in various television programs and commercials. He also gives full support to his LDS faith and appears in many LDS Church events and media programs. During the NFL season, he works as a television commentator for ESPN.

In 1993, Young created the Forever Young Foundation, which provides medical, athletic, and academic assistance for underprivileged children who have health problems.

7

The Mormon Church: From America to the World

THE CHURCH OF JESUS CHRIST OF LATTER-DAY SAINTS BEGAN THE 21st century under the leadership of President Gordon B. Hinckley (b.1910). Hinckley now leads one of the few truly global churches, with LDS congregations found in more than 200 countries (joining only Roman Catholicism, the Baha'i Faith, Seventh Day Adventists, and Jehovah's Witnesses in reaching that many nations). He took office in 1995, at age 85, succeeding the 14th LDS president, Howard William Hunter (1907–1995), who had been in office only six months when he died. Hinckley has also emerged as the most traveled LDS Church president, having logged more than a quarter of a million miles visiting members in many of the world's countries.

Hinckley has been a Church leader all of his adult life. In 1951, he became general secretary of the general missionary committee, was named to the Quorum of the Twelve Apostles in 1961, and served as first counselor to two Church presidents, Ezra Taft Benson and Hunter.

A staunch conservative, Hinckley has angered a few people in the Church, but has emerged as one of the most popular presidents in recent decades. He is known for his personal presence, his ability as a speaker, and a surprising sense of humor that emerges in the midst of his very serious messages from the pulpit.

To observers inside and outside the LDS family, the energetic Hinckley has also emerged as a symbol of the Church, embodying many of its strengths and some of the important challenges it must face if it is to remain a growing spiritual community.

A Growing Church

Hinckley oversees a growing church. The spectacular growth began under David O. McKay (see page 46), president of the Church for two decades (1950–1970). In its first 100 years the LDS Church gathered in only a million members; during McKay's presidency, it almost tripled in size. McKay did much to shape that growth by directing missionaries to new countries and by building impressive temples in Switzerland, New Zealand, suburban London, and two in California, which made the higher levels of the Mormon religious life more readily available to members.

The growth that began under McKay has continued to the present. When Hinckley took office, the Church reported 9.3 million members. As of 2002, it claims more than 11 million members. Temple construction continues, with more than 20 having been consecrated in the 1980s alone. However, during Hinckley's first seven years, the number of temples more than doubled, from 47 to 116. Included have been 11 temples in Mexico, where membership is above 900,000. Temples are now found across Europe and North America, and as far away as Fiji, Australia, Korea, Hong Kong, South Africa, and Argentina.

Spurring the Church's growth has been the translation of materials, especially the Book of Mormon, into languages other than English. Complete editions of the Book of Mormon now exist in more than 35 languages, including an English Braille edition for the blind and partial translations in many more languages. The creation of a multilingual church is supported by a large language studies curriculum at Brigham Young University and a welcoming atmosphere in the state of Utah to those who speak languages other than English. Utah begins the 21st century with a population that speaks more of the world's languages than any other state.

The emphasis on foreign languages in the public schools paid off for Utah during the 2002 Olympics, when a large number of young people, conversant in the world's major languages, were assigned to assist journalists and visitors to the Church's showcase buildings in Salt Lake

The head man
Gordon Hinckley (right), president and prophet of the Mormon Church, is the public face of the LDS Church. He is seen here being interviewed on CNN by Larry King.

City. The Olympics came off with relatively few hitches and became a major worldwide public relations event not just for the state of Utah, but for the LDS Church.

Leadership Challenges

The growth of the Church has been dramatic. It is now one of the 10 largest denominations in the United States, ahead of such older denominations as the Episcopal Church, the United Church of Christ, and the Presbyterian Church (USA). And, unlike most of the older churches, the Church of Jesus Christ of Latter-day Saints continues to grow. That growth, of course, has brought the Church a high profile that is in sharp contrast to the very negative image it had in the 19th century as the "polygamy church."

That high profile has also made it an object of public scrutiny, especially in relation to Mormon stances that have appeared to be out of step with major trends in national life. The Civil Rights movement focused the spotlight on the Church's racial policies, and contributed to the opening of the priesthood to non-white members. Another factor in that change was that the majority of Mormons now live outside the United States.

However, in spite of the changes in priesthood policy and the growth of non-American membership, changes have yet to be reflected in the higher policy-making arenas of Church leadership. The First Presidency and Quorum of the Twelve Apostles are all white American males, and the same is nearly true for the second echelon of leadership. Non-American members of The Seventy began to grow in the 1990s, but they remain a distinct minority.

The other issue remaining to be faced by the leadership is the increasing pressure from female members to participate in the Church's leadership. Currently, female leadership is limited to the Church's women's auxiliary organizations, such as the Relief Society, the Primary, and Young Women. The Church has been among the leading

Spanning the globe
The Mormon Church continues to be one of the fastest-growing worldwide, thanks in no small part to the work of missionaries such as this young man in Moscow talking with Russians about the Book of Mormon.

organizations to argue for traditional roles for women as wives and mothers. It actively opposed the Equal Rights Amendment and has excommunicated outspoken feminists (see page 94).

The Church's position on women has developed out of the abandonment of polygamy and the elevation of the nuclear family to center stage. It has adopted a program of support for family life and looks to its male leaders as models of faithful wage-earners, husbands, and fathers.

The role assigned nuclear families in Mormon life has also had repercussions on its gay and lesbian members, who have been excommunicated when they reveal their sexual orientation.

The leadership of the Church by white males almost exclusively will continue to raise issues, although for the immediate future the Church has been content to accept the losses that will come as its liberal wing is alienated by its conservative stance. The majority of members have given the Church spirited support. It is no surprise to find the majority of Mormons in the United States support the Republican Party, which shares many of the Church's conservative social views on family.

Dealing with the Image Issue

The Church of Jesus Christ of Latter-day Saints emerged as the first of what would be hundreds of American-born religious communities. It is by far the most successful, but its early success came as it gathered many socially alienated or economically outcast people from mainstream society, who were willing to try the Mormon experiment in religion and community building. With the demise of polygamy, the incorporation of Utah into the United States, and the acceptance of the first senators and congressmen from Mormon lands into the national legislature, the thrust of the Church changed considerably. The idea of building a Mormon Empire in the American West dissolved. Integration and acceptance into American life became the goal.

During the 19th century, Mormon pioneers settled many corners of the American West and founded communities that in the 20th century grew into large metropolitan areas. These former Mormon areas became increasingly pluralistic, and currently even Salt Lake City is home to the same array of churches and religious groups as other American cities.

The drive to become mainstream Americans, to be accepted as just another leaf in the American salad bowl, so to speak, has its obstacles. Not the least of the problems have come from older Christian denominations that continue to oppose the Latter-day Saints because of their many differences from Christian orthodoxy. And while most of those churches have withdrawn support for anti-Mormon activities and propaganda, several hundred small independent ministries, most identified with the Evangelical Christian community, keep up an attack on the LDS Church. A flood of books and pamphlets are produced annually that challenge Mormon beliefs, question the integrity of the Mormon scriptures, and call into question the work of Joseph Smith.

Responding to the many critics, in 1979 a group of Mormon intellectuals founded the Foundation for Ancient Research and Mormon Studies (popularly known as FARMS), which set as its task the defense of the faith through research and publications about the Book of Mormon. In 1997, FARMS merged into Brigham Young University. In 2001 BYU established the Institute for the Study and Preservation of Ancient Religious Texts, which merged FARMS' efforts with related work by its own faculty.

The Institute has emerged as the major voice of a traditional and literal understanding of the Mormon past, which includes the attempt to locate archaeological remains that would verify the history related in the Book of Mormon about life in ancient America. FARMS and Institute literature has joined the modest amount of literature produced by the LDS Church to both answer its critics and train its youthful missionaries, who must encounter the critics as they go about their duties day to day.

Overcoming the critics has become part of the Mormon program of gaining acceptance in the larger culture. Accompanying this has been an equally important battle within the Church over its own self-image. How is the Church to be seen in relation to the larger Christian community? At one level, members have attempted to create an image of the LDS Church as just another Christian variation, with little more difference from mainstream Christianity than Methodists differs from Lutherans or Presbyterians differ from Episcopalians. In very practical areas, especially when it comes to community service, Mormons now work side-by-side with social workers from a wide spectrum of churches.

This drive to be seen as just another Christian church has been evident during Hinckley's presidency. He has begun a program to further integrate the LDS Church into the mainstream and has called upon members and observers alike to stop referring to the Church as Mormons and even as Latter-day Saints, but simply as the Church of Jesus Christ. This perspective is reflected in the Church's web site and official news releases (although no attempt has yet been made to change the name of the Mormon Tabernacle Choir).

At the same time, an attempt has been made to see the Church as having a distinctive place regarding the Christian word, with much LDS literature viewing the Church as a further revelation of God, much as Christianity saw itself as a further revelation of God relative to Judaism. The implication of this position, also supported by Church leadership, is that the LDS Church is a different religion altogether, distinct from both Judaism and Christianity. While seemingly two very contradictory views, in practice many members appear able to comfortably live with both ideas.

A Way to Be American

The Church of Jesus Christ of Latter-day Saints is a homegrown American church that has found a way to be American by affirming the freedom to be different—a freedom Americans value deeply. Their way includes an affirmation of national life and patriotism, including full participation in national debates on issues from abortion to the war on terrorism. The Church has made common cause with conservative voices calling for a strong national defense effort, the centrality of the family, and the need for personal responsibility. Church leaders took their place in dealing with the national tragedy after September 11, 2002, when the Pentagon and the World Trade Center were attacked by terrorists, joining in the call for comfort for victims and supporting national efforts to defend America from future attacks.

While keeping its distinctive positions, the LDS Church affirms shared Christian values and common Christian symbols. It challenges other religious communities to build strong youth programs, fund and maintain social support agencies, and work to bring sacredness into the wider culture. Although it continues to create a culture that many Americans either question or envy, the LDS Church has made a unique place for itself in American life that appears to be firmly established.

A SCIENTIFIC ISSUE

In May 2002, Thomas Murphy, a Mormon who is an anthropologist at Edmonds (Washington) Community College, published an article that called into question a key fact from the Book of Mormon. Murphy used DNA research to show that Native Americans were not, as Mormons believe, descended from a lost tribe of Israel, the Lamanites. As this book was going to press, LDS officials were considering excommunicating Murphy for his views.

This is not the first time Mormons have challenged the literal truth of the Book of Mormon, but it is the first time such detailed scientific research had been used.

In a December 7, 2002, article in the *Seattle Times*, Murphy said, "There's a group of Mormon scholars, which includes me, that believe that the scientific and historical evidence against the historical claims in the Book of Mormon is so overwhelming that it's time to openly discuss the possibility of viewing the Book of Mormon as fiction, but inspired fiction."

Mormon scholars disagree with Murphy and point to ways that genetic markers from ancient peoples might have been lost over the millennia.

GLOSSARY

Aaronic Priesthood The lower order of priests in the Church of Jesus Christ of Latter-day Saints into which all male members are inducted, usually before their 18th birthday. It allows them to teach, preach, and baptize converts.

apostasy The act of denying a faith once held, an act which is often followed by open opposition to the community that adheres to that faith.

branch A local congregation in the LDS, usually with 200 or fewer members. Larger congregations are called wards. Branches are usually seen as growing into wards.

celestial kingdom The highest of three levels of heaven in the afterlife, according to Mormons. It is open to believers who have been baptized and entered into a marriage with the sealing ceremony conducted in a Latter-day Saints temple.

disfellowship A temporary suspension of membership in the Church that denies Church benefits to a member who is leading an outwardly sinful life or who has expressed views contrary to the stated teachings of the Church.

endowment Power from God to do one's sacred work in the world and strength not to fall away from the truth. Members of the LDS Church believe that, following a period of instruction, they may be given endowment in the temple services. Among the privileges of receiving one's endowment is being allowed to be baptized on behalf of one's relations long deceased, who never heard the message of the LDS Church.

exaltation Salvation in the highest degree. Latter-day Saints believe that ultimately some Church members may become like God.

excommunication Permanent removal from membership in the church, because someone is leading an outwardly sinful life or has expressed views contrary to the stated teachings of the LDS Church.

fast To refrain from taking food and/or liquid for purposes of self-examination, rededication of one's life, or a deeper experience of God.

genealogy A record of one's physical ancestors. Because of their belief that one can assist ancestors to attain a heaven place by being baptized in their stead, Mormons have become some of the most accomplished genealogists and keepers of genealogical records.

Great Awakening The name of several periods in American history in which a general wave of religious enthusiasm swept through the public. The First Great Awakening began in the 1740s and the Second at the beginning of the 19th century. The Latter-day Saints community is usually seen as a product of the Second Great Awakening.

Latter-day Saints Literally, those believers called to faith in response to the approaching end of the present order of things. Specifically, the term applies to members of the Church of Jesus Christ of Latter-day Saints, who believe themselves to be living at the end of the Christian era just before Christ's return to establish the kingdom of God.

manifesto A public declaration of intention or plan of action. Among Mormons, the most prominent manifesto was that issued in 1890 by Church president Wilford Woodruff that ended polygamy.

Melchizedek Priesthood The higher level of priesthood in the LDS Church. The Melchizedek priesthood confers the privilege and authority to act in the name of Christ and to organize and/or direct a particular part of that work.

Mormon The name of a character in the Book of Mormon who is an ancient historian. Non-members of the LDS Church made the name synonymous with all members of the Church. Although present-day LDS members prefer the name Saints, longtime usage has made Mormons the more popular term.

Moroni The angel who, Latter-day Saints believe, appeared to Joseph Smith and directed him to the golden plates from which the Book of Mormon was translated.

mission A time set aside to go to a place far from home, usually a foreign land, where Church members will devote their time to contacting people and teaching them about the LDS Church and its beliefs. Members of the LDS Church believe it is their obligation to spread the message of Christ as they understand it. In that effort, most young men and many young women will set aside a year or two of their life to go on a mission.

plural marriage Marriage to more than one spouse at the same time. In the 19th century., Mormons practiced polygamy (in which one man marries two or more women), but not polyandry (in which one woman marries multiple men).

polygamy The marriage of one man to more than one woman.

Quorum of the Twelve Apostles The second highest authority in the LDS Church. It consists of 12 men, all previously ordained into the Melchizedek Priesthood. They operate under the first presidency, consisting of the Church's president and his two counselors.

Reformation A 16th-century period during which the Protestant movement was established; so-called because Protestants saw themselves as reforming the Christian Church under the authority of the Bible. Most of the first generation of Latter-day Saints had been Protestants.

restoration The Latter-day Saints see their church as a restoration of the Christian Church of the first century, which they believe had been lost over the centuries.

Sabbath The seventh day of the week, set aside in the Bible as a day of rest and worship. Most Christians, including Latter-day saints, celebrate the Sabbath on Sunday.

salvation A state of being redeemed from one's sins, which have estranged one from God. Christians believe that salvation is the result of participation in the Christian community, although they differ on exactly what that means.

sealing In the LDS Church, it is believed that marriages may be created for this earthly life, but through a special ceremony conducted only in Mormon temples, a couple may be sealed (married) for all eternity.

sects The various divisions in a religious community. Sects are distinguished by their holding to one or more distinctive beliefs and/or practices.

stake A district in the LDS Church consisting of some 3,000 or more members, who may be divided into five to 12 congregations (wards).

telestial One of the three levels of the heavenly afterlife.

temple Mormon temples are special places for services to which only members in good standing in the LDS Church are admitted. Included in these services are sealings (marriages) in which a couple takes vows to remain a family unit for all eternity, baptism for one's ancestors, and reception of one's endowment.

terrestrial One of the three levels of the heavenly afterlife.

tithing The practice of donating 10 percent of one's income to God's service. Members of the LDS Church are expected to tithe their income to the Church and its ministry.

Urim and Thummim An instrument through which it is believed revelation from God may be received. Joseph Smith claimed to have had such an instrument, which he used to assist him in translating the Book of Mormon. He described it as two stones set in a bow attached to a breastplate.

ward A local congregation consisting of from 300 to 600 individuals. Smaller congregations are designated branches.

word of wisdom A set of instructions given by Joseph Smith concerning how Mormons should live their lives.

TIME LINE

1820	First vision of Joseph Smith, Jr.
1823	Joseph Smith has a vision of the angel Moroni.
1827	Joseph Smith receives gold plates from Moroni containing the sacred texts of the Book of Mormon.
1830	The Church of Christ is founded on April 6; the Book of Mormon is published in May.
1836	First Church of Christ temple opens in Kirtland, Ohio.
1838	The Mormons leave Ohio, move to Missouri, and change their name to the Church of Jesus Christ of Latter-day Saints (LDS).
1839	The Mormons leave Missouri and move to Nauvoo, Illinois.
1844	Joseph Smith and Hyrum Smith are killed on June 27.
1847	The Mormons arrive in Salt Lake City on July 24; Brigham Young is recognized as prophet on December 27.
1852	A revelation that polygamy is no longer to be practiced is announced publicly, although the practice continues.
1857	The Mountain Meadows Massacre occurs on September 11.
1862	The U.S. Congress makes polygamy illegal.
1890	The Manifesto declares the end of polygamy.
1893	The Salt Lake Temple in Salt Lake City, Utah, is finished and dedicated.
1928	The Mormon Tabernacle Choir begins weekly radio broadcasts.
1930	Women's blessings and ordinances are forbidden.
1976	The LDS Church reaffirms its anti-abortion policy.
1978	A revelation opens LDS priesthood to men of all races.
1997	The LDS Church reenacts the 1847 Pioneer Trek.

RESOURCES

Reading List

The Book of Mormon, The Church of Jesus Christ of Latter-day Saints, 1981.

Bushman, Claudia L. and Richard L. Bushman, *Building the Kingdom: A History of Mormons in America.* New York: Oxford University Press, 1999.

Hill, Donna, *Joseph Smith: the First Mormon.* New York: Doubleday, 1977.

Hug, Dean, *The Mormon Church: A Basic History.* Salt Lake City, Utah: Deseret Books, 1986.

Johanson, W.F. Walker, *What Is Mormonism All About?* New York: St. Martin's/Griffin, 2002.

Slaughter, William, *Trail of Hope.* Salt Lake City: Deseret Books, 1997.

Swinton, Heidi S., *American Prophet: The Story of Joseph Smith.* Salt Lake City: Shadow Mountain, 1999.

Resources on the Web

On the Mormon Trail
www.americanwest.com/trails/pages/mormtrl.htm
A brief history of the westward pioneer movement by the Mormons in the 1840s and 1850s, featuring numerous photographs and paintings.

Official Church Site
www.lds.org
Contains hundreds of links to information about Mormon history, personalities, temples, beliefs, and much more.

Mormon Genealogy
www.familysearch.org
Access the 35 million names in the LDS Church genealogy archives and learn about other ways to research family history on the web.

The West
www.pbs.org/weta/thewest/program/
While not specifically about the Mormons, the site, based on a 1996 public television program, is a great way to help understand the context of the Mormons' beginnings and migration to the West in the 1800s.

INDEX

Note: *Italic* page numbers refer to illustrations.